DUGORT, ACHILL ISI

Maynooth Studies in Irish Local History

SERIES EDITOR   Raymond Gillespie

This is one of six new pamphlets in the Maynooth Studies in Irish Local History Series to be published in the year 2001 which brings the number published to forty. Like their predecessors most of the pamphlets are based on theses completed as part of the M.A. in local history programme in National University of Ireland, Maynooth. While the regions and time span which they cover are diverse, from Cork city to Tyrone, they all share a conviction that the exploration of the local past can shed light on the evolution of modern societies. They each demonstrate that understanding the evolution of local societies is important. The local worlds of Ireland in the past are as complex and sophisticated as the national framework in which they are set. The communities which peopled those local worlds, whether they be the inhabitants of large cities, housing on the edge of those cities or rural estates, shaped and were shaped by their environments to create a series of inter-locking worlds of considerable complexity. Those past worlds are best interpreted not through local administrative divisions, such as the county, but in human units: local places where communities of people lived and died. Untangling what held these communities together, and what drove them apart, gives us new insights into the world we have lost.

These pamphlets each make a significant contribution to understanding Irish society in the past. Together with thirty-four earlier works in this series they explore something of the hopes and fears of those who lived in Irish local communities in the past. In doing so they provide examples of the practice of local history at its best and show the vibrant discipline which the study of local history in Ireland has become in recent years.

Maynooth Studies in Irish Local History: Number 39

Dugort, Achill Island, 1831–61

*A study of the rise and fall of a
missionary community*

Mealla C. Ní Ghiobúin

IRISH ACADEMIC PRESS
DUBLIN • PORTLAND, OR

First published in 2001 by
IRISH ACADEMIC PRESS
44, Northumberland Road, Dublin 4, Ireland
and in the United States of America by
IRISH ACADEMIC PRESS
c/o ISBS, 5824 NE Hassalo Street, Portland, OR 97213–3644.

website: www.iap.ie

British Library Cataloguing in Publication Data
Ghiobuin, Mealla C. Ni
  Dugort, Achill Island, 1831–1861: a study of the rise and fall of a missionary
  community. – (Maynooth studies in Irish local history; no. 39)
  1. Missionary settlements – Ireland – Dugort – History – 19th century 2. Dugort
  (Ireland) – History – 19th century 3. Dugort (Ireland) – Social life and customs
  – 19th century
  I. Title
  941.7'081
  ISBN 0–7165–2740–5

A catalog record of this book is available from the Library of Congress

Typeset in 10 pt on 12 pt Bembo by
Carrigboy Typesetting Services, County Cork
Printed by Creative Print and Design (Wales) Ebbw Vale

Contents

FIGURES

TABLES

Acknowledgements

In the course of my research for this study, the staff of the the following institutions gave me great assistance - the National Archives of Ireland, the National Library of Ireland, the NUI Maynooth Library, the Gilbert Library, the Valuation Office, Dublin, the British Library, London, the Representative Church Body Library, Dublin, the Royal Irish Academy, and the Irish Church Missions, Dublin.

Rev. Gary Hastings, rector of Holy Trinity Church, Westport, provided me with access to the parish registers and other records of the Church of St Thomas, Dugort. On Achill Island, among those who were of particular assistance were Mrs. Vi McDowell of Gray's Guest House, Dugort and John O'Shea of Dooagh. In Dublin, my special thanks go to Bill Bolger and Niamh O'Sullivan for their invaluable assistance.

Dr Raymond Gillespie, the course director of the MA in Local History, provided a wonderfully stimulating programme of studies over the two years of the course. I am greatly indebted to Dr Gillespie, who was my MA supervisor, for his assistance, patience, much valued advice and encouragement.

The support and friendship of my fellow students in Maynooth, 1998-2000, was greatly appreciated.

Finally, my thanks to Seamus and Phil for all their help and encouragement.

Introduction

Achill Island is the largest of Ireland's offshore islands. It has an area of fifty-seven square miles, measuring fifteen miles from east to west and eleven miles from north to south, narrowing to eight miles at Keel. The Sound (sea channel) which separates the island from the mainland enabled the passage of shipping without the necessity of making the long and hazardous journey around Achill Head.[1] Before 1887 when a bridge was built across the Sound by the surveyor, Patrick Chalmers Cowan, the island was isolated from the rest of County Mayo.[2] Up to that time access to this remote island depended on the tides and the weather.

Two-thirds of the island of Achill is covered by peat, mainly at its centre, while a large portion of the coastal arable land is cultivated peat or soil. There are some small lakes on the island but virtually no trees. The highest mountain is Slievemore (2,214 feet). There are no large towns but rather a number of coastal village settlements, the principal being Dooagh, Keel, Achill Sound and Dugort. Dugort (its name means black field) is situated on the northern coast, under the shadow of the Slievemore mountain. Until the early nineteenth century, there were no roads on the island and the main access, as has already been noted, was by sea. In the report on public works in the Western District, in 1828, Alexander Nimmo wrote

> Newport into Achill Island – This road is completed as far as the Sound, though the portion of old country road next Newport would require considerable amendment. I had suspended the part within the island, though very near completion, except so far as to complete a path for horses into the centre of the island; but it is painful to see the poor people carrying their corn on men and women's backs over the cliffs of 1,500 feet high, and along a wild track of mountain, bog and strand to get at the line which has thus been opened; and I know no part of my district which would sooner rise in consequence than this, if once laid open by roads.[3]

Nimmo's description gives some idea of the physical conditions prevailing on the island in the early years of the nineteenth century when a Protestant missionary settlement was established at Dugort. In the early part of that century, between 5,000 and 6,000 people lived on the island. The religious census of 1834 reported that of these only seventy-six, mostly coastguard men,

1. Map of Achill Island taken from Samuel Lewis, *Atlas of Ireland*, (London 1837), also showing Inishbegil (Inishbiggle) and Clare islands. (Source: RIA).

2. Location of villages mentioned in the text (drawn by M.C. Ní Ghiobúin).

their families, and persons connected with relief committees, were Protestant.[4] The majority were Irish speaking and Roman Catholic. Achill was originally included in the Protestant parish of Burrishoole, but owing to some visitation entries, the archbishop considered it a distinct parish and on dissolving the union of Newport in July 1830 he presented the supposed rectory, as an honourable superannuation to Rev. Charles Wilson, an old curate, whom he found in the union. 'The income was not above £100 per annum – there was no cure of souls – no Protestant congregation – no church – and no glebe.'[5] This was the state of the Protestant parish of Achill before the advent of the Achill Mission.

The Achill missionary settlement at Dugort (or 'colony' as it is known even to this day) was established in the early 1830s during a period of intense activity by a number of Protestant evangelicals, who were 'convinced that it was their religious duty to free Irish Catholics from "popish superstition" and the authority of the Anti-Christ in Rome.'[6] The Achill Mission, founded by the Rev. Edward Nangle, was not unique but was part of the wider movement by evangelicals to convert the Roman Catholic population along the western seaboard of Ireland, through the medium of their own language, to the Protestant faith. Underlying this movement was a serious attempt to change the nature of the existing peasant culture, which was both Roman Catholic and

Irish. At the time, Irish evangelicals were combining ideas of evangelicalism and imperialism and pursuing a proselytising policy among the Irish Catholics which sought to bring them the twofold blessings of a reformed faith and British civilisation.[7]

The Achill Mission was only one of a number of proselytising attempts at converting the Roman Catholic population. Two other settlements, at Dingle, County Kerry and in Connemara, County Galway, were also founded for the same purpose, but while they thrived for a time, neither had the same 'success' or notoriety as that achieved by the Achill Mission at Dugort. One of the characteristics of these settlements was their ability to create controversy by stirring up resentment between them and the local Catholic clergy. The publicity which followed each incident led to very considerable funds flowing in the direction of the missions, mainly from sympathisers in England.

The period chosen for this study of the Achill missionary settlement at Dugort is from 1831 to 1861. The main players in this nineteenth century experiment were the Rev. Edward Nangle, his friend, Neason Adams, M.D., honorary physician to the Mission, Sir Richard O'Donnel, landlord of most of Achill Island, the Irish Society which supplied and paid for scripture readers with a knowledge of Irish, and the Irish Church Missions which was involved in efforts to keep the Mission going when it ran into financial difficulties. The Protestant archbishop of Tuam, Dr Power le Poer Trench, a fervent evangelical, was an enthusiastic supporter of Edward Nangle and the Achill Mission. Opposed to the Mission and all its activities was the Roman Catholic archbishop of Tuam, Dr John MacHale who sent a succession of militant priests to the island in an effort to thwart any progress on the part of the Mission.

The historian, H.P.R. Finberg maintained that it was the business of the local historian to re-enact for the reader the 'origin, growth, decline and fall of a community.'[8] The history of the Achill missionary settlement represents a classic example of this definition, and its story is told here. A wide range of sources was used in the preparation of this study. One of the major sources of information about the Rev. Edward Nangle and the Achill Mission is the biography written by Rev. Henry Seddall, LL.D. His book, *Edward Nangle, the apostle of Achill: a memoir and a history*, with an introduction by the Most Rev. Lord Plunket, D.D., bishop of Tuam, was published in 1884, the year after Nangle's death. Seddall, who was rector of Vastina, in the diocese of Meath, and also a member of the Achill Mission committee for the previous four years, was given access to Nangle's diaries and papers. From this point of view it is a very important and contemporary record of the Achill Mission. However, another view is that given by the Rev. James Greer in his book *The windings of the Moy with Skreen and Tireragh*. Greer, a graduate of Trinity College Dublin, and an ex-rector retired, spent from 1863–5 in the training school founded by Edward Nangle in Skreen, County Sligo, in preparation for Kildare Place, now the Church of Ireland training college. He commented that

Dr Seddall has written a book, narrow and prejudiced, and just fitting for whom he wrote. However, he has managed to collect the salient events in the life of the Great Nangle. Were it not for this book, the apostle of Achill, the benefactor of Skreen, the renowned controversialist of Ireland for half a century would be clean forgotten like the dead, out of mind.[9]

In dealing with the history of the Achill Mission, two other sources stand out. The first is the monthly journal which was published by the Achill Mission from 1837 to the late 1860s, after which it had a name change. This was the *Achill Missionary Herald and Western Witness* or, as it is commonly referred to, the *Achill Herald*. Edward Nangle was the editor of and main contributor to this journal and he used it as a vehicle for the dissemination of his ideas, to counteract any criticism of either his methods or of the settlement, to provoke controversy, and also to appeal for funds for the support of the settlement and its activities.

The *Annual Reports* of the Achill Mission are another important contemporary source. These were also written by Nangle. Only eight of these reports have survived and they relate for the most part to the years 1835–50. Unfortunately, reports for the years 1845–7 are missing, otherwise they might have revealed valuable information about the Famine years. There is also a statement issued by the Achill committee in January 1858, which, while not an annual report, is nevertheless a useful point of reference. All the reports provide details of activities under three headings – temporal, education and the ministry of the Gospel.

The information contained in the *Achill Herald* and the written parts of the *Annual Reports* have to be treated with a certain amount of caution bearing in mind their original intended audience. The missionary settlement was almost completely dependant for its support and continuance on voluntary subscriptions, and it was of the utmost importance that such contributions continued to flow. The Mission could never have survived, in spite of the best efforts on the part of its managers, on what it could produce itself.

Official census records, especially from 1841 onwards, the parish registers of births, marriages and burials for Dugort, and Griffith's valuation[10] all provide information about the people who lived in the area. The National Archives holds outrage papers dealing with crime in Mayo, as well as the distress and relief papers for the period of the Famine, and these are valuable sources for the mid-nineteenth century. The Famine had a profound effect on the Mission, which was like an oasis in a desert, with its fertile crops, while all around was starvation and misery. Undoubtedly, the efforts of the missionaries helped save many lives, but the accusation, especially against Nangle, of using the Famine as an opportunity to make further converts to Protestantism, remains to this day.

There are also a number of contemporary descriptions of the settlement written by visitors. Two in particular are of interest and both were extremely critical of what they found there. The Victorian travel writers, Mr and Mrs Samuel Carter Hall, visited the settlement in 1842 and again in 1849. Their book, *Ireland: its scenery and character*, published in 1843, provides an account of their visit. Mrs Asenath Nicholson recorded her impressions in two books, *Ireland's welcome to the stranger: or, excursions through Ireland in 1844 and 1845 for the purpose of personally investigating the condition of the poor*, and the later *Lights and shades of Ireland*, published in 1850 after her second visit. However, as in the case of the author of the *Achill Herald* and *Annual Reports*, the motives of these and other contemporary writers, of which there are a number, must be taken into consideration as it is likely that most of them would have sought to influence their intended readers.

Desmond Bowen's *The Protestant crusade in Ireland, 1800–70: a study of Protestant-Catholic relations between the Act of Union and Disestablishment*, and, *Souperism: myth or reality, a study in souperism* (published in the 1970s), provide a background to the religious conflicts of the time, including the spread of the 'Second Reformation' and the work of the evangelicals. The place of the Achill Mission in all of this is explored in both books. Irene Whelan's 'Edward Nangle and the Achill Mission, 1834–52', gives a valuable assessment of this period. This essay is part of a collection entitled *A various country, essays in Mayo history 1500–1900*, published in 1987.

This present study illustrates the background to the foundation of the Mission, the administrative framework and management of the settlement, and the opposition to it in its formative years. It shows how the settlement evolved between 1833 and the beginning of the Famine in 1845. In the aftermath of the Famine, the Mission sought to consolidate its leased holdings by purchasing in 1850–1 Sir Richard O'Donnel's Achill estate through the Encumbered Estates Court. The Achill Mission then became the owner of two-thirds of the island. This major expansion led to serious financial difficulties and the almost total collapse of the Mission from which it was rescued, for a short period, by the Irish Church Missions.

The departure of Edward Nangle for Skreen in County Sligo in 1852 and the absence of his managerial skills, together with the falling off of voluntary contributions and the lack of return on its investment, all hastened the decline and the ultimate demise of the Mission.

Beginnings

Edward Nangle was the descendant of an ancient Catholic family of Anglo-Norman stock. The origins of the family can be traced back to the twelfth century. Edward Nangle's father, Walter, a Catholic, was married three times. His first and third wives were Catholics but his second wife, Edward's mother, was a Protestant. She died when Edward was nine years of age.[1] Whether she had a dominant influence on his religious outlook is not certain but she may have laid the foundation for his subsequent adherence to a very rigid form of evangelicalism. Edward was born in either 1799 or 1800[2] in Kildalkey near Athboy in County Meath. He graduated with a BA from Trinity College, Dublin in 1823 and entered the ministry of the Church of Ireland, being ordained a deacon in 1824 by the bishop of Meath, Right Rev. Dr Thomas O'Beirne, on the nomination to the curacy of Athboy.[3] He was subsequently admitted to priest's orders by the bishop of Kilmore, the Right Rev. Dr George Beresford. He remained only a few months in Athboy before moving to Monkstown, County Dublin where he fulfilled a temporary appointment. At the age of twenty-four he received an appointment to the diocese of Kilmore and the parish of Arva on the borders of Cavan and Longford.[4] It was here that he became deeply influenced by the local Primitive Church Methodists. He also met Rev. William Krause, who was 'moral' agent to the Cavan landlord, Lord Farnham. Farnham was involved in that revival of Protestantism in Ireland known as the 'Second Reformation.' Krause turned Nangle's beliefs towards evangelicalism.[5] Two years of strenuous work among the parishioners led to a complete breakdown of his health. Owing to this and the fact that his father's circumstances were reduced, he resigned the curacy in Arva.[6]

Nangle was an occasional visitor to Athboy and to Dr James Adams who introduced him to his brother Dr Neason Adams, who later became the mainstay of the Achill Mission.[7] After leaving Arva, Nangle spent the next twelve months in the house of Dr Neason Adams in Dublin where he was nursed with the greatest care and where he had the best medical advice provided for him.[8] Altogether he spent about five years trying to improve his health. It was also a time of comparative poverty as he was without any clerical appointment, possibly due to his past record and to his known leanings towards evangelicalism. His father too was unable to assist him as he had fallen on hard times. During this period he studied the Irish language.[9] After two years, he was appointed secretary to the Sunday School Society for

3. Reverend Edward Nangle, founder of the missionary settlement at Dugort, Achill.

Ireland, shortly afterwards exchanging this for another post as literary assistant to the Religious Tract Society, selling penny pamphlets from door to door.[10] In September 1828, he married his first wife, Elizabeth (Eliza) Warner of Marvelstown House, near Kells, County Meath, whom he first met at the house of Dr James Adams in Athboy.[11] She was the eldest daughter of Henry Warner and his wife Patience (nee Biddulph).[12]

In 1831, the western part of Connacht, particularly Mayo and Sligo, suffered severely from famine, the result of disastrous winds which destroyed the potato crop.[13] An outbreak of cholera also swept the area.[14] Evangelical friends asked Edward and Elizabeth Nangle and the rector of Durrus, near Bantry, County Cork, Rev. James Freke, to accompany the steamer *Nottingham* from Dublin to Westport with a cargo of Indian meal and to report on the condition of the peasantry, believed to be starving, along the Mayo coast.[15] They left Dublin on a Saturday evening and after a very stormy passage near Achill, got to Westport the following Wednesday evening.[16] Before they left the boat, the Rev. William Baker Stoney, at that time rector of Newport and afterwards for many years of Castlebar, came on board to claim a portion of the cargo for distribution to those starving in his parish. They spent the night with Rev. Stoney who suggested to Edward Nangle that he should visit Achill Island.[17] Rev. Stoney was later to become a member of the Achill Mission committee.[18] From Westport, they travelled to Newport where they stayed overnight.

The next day, Nangle, mounted on a pony and accompanied by a scripture reader, set out from Newport for Achill Sound where they arrived late that evening. On the way they visited some cabins and found the people in an appalling state of destitution.[19] At that time, there was no regular ferry boat between the island and the mainland, and no piers on either side, and the only buildings visible were two roofless houses. They were told that there had been an abortive attempt to establish a salt factory there. They spent the night with a respectable widow who had no English.[20] The following morning, Nangle and his companion crossed the Sound on the sand when the tide was out. As there was no road, they made their way, on foot, by a horse track which wound around a very rugged coast and which led them to the coastguard station at Bullsmouth where they were entertained by the chief officer. This journey of about seven miles took them all day.[21] Until the beginning of the nineteenth century wheeled transport was virtually unknown in Achill and there was scarcely a stretch of road that could justifiably be described as such. The most primitive of 'roads' connecting one area of village settlement with another or giving access to turf cutting, were little more than single file paths.[22] The following day, they visited Dugort and also went further west to Keel.[23]

According to Nangle, he had for a long time decided to devote himself to missionary work among the native Irish on the plan of the United Brethren (Moravians) and he saw Achill as the ideal setting for such an endeavour. He returned to Newport after a few days to discuss with Rev. Stoney how best to achieve his purpose.[24] He was introduced to Sir Richard O'Donnel who owned most of Achill Island and whose seat was Newport House in Newport. Sir Richard assured Nangle that he would use all his influence to advance the enterprise and promised to give him for the benefit of the proposed mission a tract of 130 acres of land for a nominal rent and for the longest lease he could give, which was for a period of three lives or thirty-one years.[25]

Following this visit to Achill, Nangle returned to Dublin and began making preparations for the setting up of his mission. He contacted the Rev. Robert Daly to enlist his support.[26] It was likely that Nangle had a previous acquaintance with Daly who was a nephew of Lord Farnham, the Cavan landowner. At that time, Daly, a well-known Protestant militant, was rector of Powerscourt in County Wicklow.[27] He was also acknowledged as an Irish evangelical leader, was proficient in the Irish language and took a deep interest in the native Irish.[28] In 1843, Daly became bishop of Cashel.[29] He expressed his approval of Nangle's plans, and, as he traced out on a map of Ireland the locality where it was intended to establish the missionary settlement, said he had often traversed the principal part of it 'at a time when he thought that God had sent

him into the world for no higher purpose than to murder grouse.'[30] Daly asked
that he be entered on the subscription list for the missionary enterprise, which
had recently been opened, and immediately gave a contribution of £50.[31]

However, Nangle, writing in 1864, said he did not receive similar encouragement from all he contacted about his mission. He said many regarded it 'a
wild speculation, originating in a romantic imagination, and which would be
soon abandoned when the difficulties connected with its accomplishment came
to be grappled with.' He went on to say that 'one old gentleman, who by clever
management and thrift, and pliant subserviency to men in high stations, had
succeeded in raising himself to a high position of wealth and influence, whenever
he heard of the Achill Mission spoken of, used to turn up his eyes and raise his
hands to say, "in nubibus, sir, in nubibus."'[32] Other views expressed were those of
personal friends who said he had no right to sacrifice the interests of his family
by engaging in an enterprise which cut off all prospects of professional advance-
ment. Some of his Christian friends also endeavoured to discourage him from
proceeding with his purpose.[33] When a popular evangelical minister asked him
why he was going on such a 'wild goose chase to that island of Achill', he replied
that 'I do not consider it to be a wild goose chase. Achill is the most destitute spot
in Ireland, and I wish to lift up the standard of the cross among its inhabitants.'
The minister replied 'I tell you, you will not be six weeks in the island until the
priests will have blown you into the Atlantic.' Nangle replied 'God is stronger
than the priests'.[34] From these quotations, it is clear that Edward Nangle did not
intend being deflected from his purpose in spite of warnings from friends and
others. We are not told what his wife thought of his intentions to move his family
to such a wild part of the country.

Nangle probably realised that he would need some sort of formal support
for the management of the intended mission. A committee was now formed
to promote the interests of the proposed missionary settlement. As Achill was
part of the diocese of Tuam, this committee wrote to the archbishop, Dr
Power le Poer Trench, outlining the plan for the mission and asking for his
sanction and support, to which the archbishop replied expressing his
enthusiasm for the project.[35] Archbishop Trench was a fervent evangelical.[36]

The next step was to obtain a lease of land for the site of the intended
missionary settlement. All the land in the area was already leased by tenants from
Sir Richard O'Donnel who were 'very determined to maintain their hold on the
land'. The tenants were induced, with great difficulty, 'to surrender their hold on
130 acres of wild mountain without any building or a rood of cultivated ground
upon it, for £90, and the committee stipulated to pay a yearly rent of £1 to the
head landlord.'[37] Nangle, in his history of the Mission, wrote that

> the only spot on this plot of ground, which presented a suitable site for
> the intended settlement, was, at the time it came into our possession, a
> swamp so soft that, to use the expression of the islanders, ' a hare could

not walk over it.' But we had no choice. No other land but this could be obtained and had the design of our purchase transpired, the influence of the priest would have been used, and doubtless successfully with the tenants, to withhold even that from us.[38]

Clearly, even at this early stage, Nangle expected opposition to his mission and took steps to avoid confrontation with the Roman Catholic clergy before it was firmly established. He later wrote that at the time the difficulties seemed almost insurmountable.[39] About this time, a sum of £390 was lodged in the bank anonymously to the credit of the Mission. Nangle later learned that this large contribution was the gift of a Christian lady, a member of a dissenting congregation in the city of Dublin.[40] In the summer of 1833, when all the legal arrangements had been completed, a steward was appointed to super- intend the reclamation of the land and the erection of some small houses.[41]

> In 1837, three years after his arrival in Dugort, Nangle wrote that a wild tract of moor overrun with heath, was to be claimed and rendered productive – houses were to be erected in the midst of the wilderness, without any means of communication with a civilized country but the sea, which in consequence of a boisterous climate, and the want of a commodious landing-place, afforded but a precarious medium of inter- course; and these works were to be accomplished by the instrumentality of a people destitute of skill or suitable implements, whose ignorance and prejudices might easily be worked upon by designing men, as to make them regard the growth of the infant settlement with jealous enmity, instead of considering it in the light of a benefit, either spiritual or temporal.

He went on

> (u)nder the superintendence of the steward, however, the farm was soon inclosed, and a house being erected sufficient for the accommodation of two families, the committee sent a schoolmaster to the settlement in November 1833, he was shortly followed by a scripture-reader and another house being erected, a clergyman, who was appointed by the committee in Dublin to take charge of the settlement as missionary, removed there with his family, in August 1834, where he was shortly followed by another minister and three more scripture readers, for whom an extensive and encouraging field of labour was opened.[42]

Here, Nangle was writing about himself and citing the committee as the authority for his legitimacy as missionary at the settlement.

According to Seddall's biography of Edward Nangle published in 1884, 'it was not until 1834 that matters were sufficiently matured for Mr Nangle's permanent sojourn at the infant settlement.'[43] He spent the intervening time in Ballina where he worked with the Church of Ireland Home Mission.[44] There is a reference to a meeting in January 1833 of the Bible Society for the northern district of Mayo held in Ballina at which Edward Nangle spoke.[45] During his stay in Ballina, his third child was born.[46] One account gave the date of his arrival on Achill as 30 July 1834, while another indicated that 'the Rev. E. Nangle came to lead the work of the Mission on Friday 1st August 1834. He arrived by boat at Dugort Bay at 10 o'clock at night to a welcome including a large bonfire on the beach.'[47]

Seddall describes the place as follows – 'one of the two small houses which had been built was inhabited by the steward, the schoolmaster, and the scripture reader, the other was assigned to Mr Nangle. It also afforded accommodation for Rev. Joseph Duncan, who had been sent by the committee in Dublin to help Mr Nangle.'[48] Rev. Joseph Baylee replaced Duncan who left the Mission in 1836 because of ill-health. 'Rev. Baylee arrived on 29 January 1836 in the midst of a storm which threatened to lay the whole settlement in ruins.'[49] According to Seddall, 'the accommodation was very limited; the inconvenience to which all had to submit was very great. Food, too, was very scanty and had to be procured'. There was no meat on the island, and Newport was the nearest market town, twenty-five miles away and for nine of these there was no road.[50]

About a year after the arrival of the missionary party on the island, the accommodation was somewhat extended. The wife of Dr Neason Adams (honorary physician to the Mission), wrote in a letter to a friend

> I am writing with my window open to allow an escape for the smoke; my hearth filled with wet sods; scarcely any fire; a big pot on a stand with rice, meal, and bones; our bed; a large horse on which clothes are spread; a shelf stuffed with a miscellaneous collection of indescribable varieties and thickly covered with ashes. Two of the rooms are converted into a printing office. Joyce and Gardiner, scripture-readers, have no other home. Lendrum, his wife and six children are all domesticated in the same house.[51]

Nangle, too, has left a description of his accommodation in the year of his arrival

> our accommodation was very limited; we had but one small room, which served me as parlour, drawing room, and study during the day, and at night it was occupied by Mr Duncan as a bed chamber, – a necessary arrangement, which was, however, attended with a double disadvantage, as Mr Duncan could not retire to rest until we vacated the apartment for the night, nor could we come down in the morning until he had risen and completed his toilet.[52]

Reference has already been made in the introduction to the *Annual Reports* of the Mission and the *Achill Missionary Herald and Western Witness* (usually referred to as the *Achill Herald*), a monthly journal begun in 1837 and published for nearly forty years. Unfortunately, only eight of the *Annual Reports*, which were written by Edward Nangle, have survived, and these were for the period between 1835 and 1850. Both of these sources provide a considerable amount of detail about the Achill Mission.

The earliest extant *Report*, the second, was published in July 1836 and covered the previous year's activities, 1835, with the following title

Second report of the Missionary Society for Achill and other islands off the Irish Coast. Published in July 1836 and printed by M Goodwin & Co., 29, Denmark Street, Dublin. The Directors of the Society were as follows:–

Rev. Denis Browne	Rev. C. Otway
Rev. E. P. Brooke	Rev. W. B. Stoney
Rev. Robert Daly	Colonel Palliser
Rev. J. D. Hastings	James Irvine, Esq.,
Rev. J. H. Singer	George Wilson, Esq.

Treasurer: Robert Newenham, Esq., Castle Street, Dublin.
Secretary: Rev. Edmund C. Pendleton, 16 Upper Sackville Street, Dublin

In the same report, there was also a list of the life members, committee and secretary of the Ladies Auxiliary Island Association. Mrs Edmund Pendleton was the secretary of this committee.[53] One of the methods of fund-raising was described in the first few pages of the report.

From an early stage of its development, the Achill Mission, through the society above-mentioned, had a wide set of contacts for raising funds for its purposes. Among the directors of the society were three well-known evangelicals, Daly, Otway and Stoney, and all of these continued to maintain an interest in the Achill Mission over a number of years. The name of the society at this time was the Missionary Society for Achill and other islands off the Irish Coast, but it is not clear when the name was changed to that of the Achill Mission.

At the beginning of the second report, Nangle apologised for the delay in furnishing it, which, although published in July 1836, covered the previous year's activities of the Mission, stating that in future it was intended to present a half-yearly statement of the society's progress instead of an annual report. It appears that this pattern of reporting was not followed as later reports were called annual reports. The report for the year 1835 was in the form of a letter from Edward Nangle to the secretary of the society and dated April 1836. He describes himself as one of the missionaries stationed on the island. Apart from the statement of accounts, the actual report was given under three headings, temporal, education and the ministry of the Gospel.[54]

Other than the naming of the directors of the society, and references to the 'committee in Dublin' sending missionaries and scripture readers to Achill, there is little information about the actual management of the Mission until the next available report, the sixth, for the year ending 31 December, 1839. This was printed at the Achill Mission Press by William Pugh, in 1840.[55]

By 1839, the missionaries, having successfully created their settlement at Dugort, now saw the advantage of having more direct control over the management of their affairs than heretofore. In the sixth report of the Mission for the year ended 31 December, 1839, Nangle gave the reasons as follows

> I must here state that since our last report the machinery of our society has undergone a new organisation. The directors in Dublin feeling that their distance from the field of operation, the slowness of commu- nication, and their limited knowledge of local circumstances, greatly hinders their efficiency in managing the Mission, have transferred their responsibility as directors to the court of local management, consisting of the two missionaries, Captain Dyer, R.N., Dr Adams, and the steward. They still continue to act as guardians of the Mission, the duties devolving upon them and us by this change in our system of management are defined in a document which will be found in the appendix; it was drawn up by one of our members and approved by our former board of directors.[56]

The rules governing the management of the Achill and Inishbiggle Mission were drawn up in January 1840 and agreed with the newly-styled board of guardians in Dublin. Hereafter, the committees are referred to in this text as the Dublin committee and the local committee respectively. Included in the rules was the obligation to keep records of subscribers as well as income and expenditure accounts, all of which were to be furnished to the Dublin committee in February each year, having first been audited. The local com- mittee members were also to meet weekly to deal with all matters relating to the Mission. (see appendix 1).

In the *9th Report,* for the year ending 31 December 1842, it was noted that the affairs of the Mission were managed by a local committee consisting of Revs. E. Nangle, E. Lowe and J. French, Captain Dyer and N. Adams, M.D., subject to the control of a board of guardians in Dublin, to whose decision all major questions, or those affecting the interests of any of the local committee, had to be referred. They met every Tuesday and Friday evenings, when all accounts were settled, and any differences which might arise among the people of the settlement were adjusted. The guardians of the Mission were as follows

Very Rev. the Dean of Ardagh	Colonel Palliser
Rev. J.H. Singer, DD., S.F.T.C.D.	Captain Phibbs
Rev. Robert Daly	Captain Irwin
Rev. Denis Browne	Rev. Thomas Kingston
Rev. W.B. Stoney	George Wilson, Esq.[57]

It is interesting to note that a number of the members of the original committee, Singer, Daly, Stoney, Browne, Palliser and Wilson, were still on the board of guardians or Dublin committee seven years later. In the *10th Annual Report* for the year ending 31 December 1843, all the same persons were still members of the board of guardians, Rev. Daly now being described as the lord bishop of Cashel. The honorary secretary of the board of guardians was Rev. T. De Vere Coneys, Irish Professor, Trinity College Dublin. Coneys had been a missionary attached to the settlement at an earlier time. The affairs of the settlement were managed by the local committee, consisting of Rev. E. Nangle, Rev. E. Lowe, T. L. Wood, Esq., and Neason Adams, M. D.[58] T. L. Wood was an inspecting officer of the coastguard who came to Achill in 1844 after serving fourteen years in Fethard, County Wexford.[59] There is no reference to the management of the Mission in the eleventh report for the year ending 31 December 1844.[60]

It can be seen from the foregoing that a level of control was imposed by the board in Dublin and that moneys received, whether in the form of subscriptions, donations, or as a result of collections, all had to be accounted for at least annually. However, on examining the printed accounts which accompanied the annual reports, one can agree with the criticism of two contemporary visitors, Mr and Mrs S.C. Hall, that they are very confusing. The Halls, who were well-known Victorian travel writers, first visited the island in 1841 and recorded their views in *Ireland; its scenery, and character.*[61] They were extremely critical of the Mission and its activities. They referred to a report of the activities of the Mission which they described as a

> very confusing document – four or five distinct separate modes of collecting money. The first is for the Mission, the second for the Orphan Asylum, the third for the Dispensary, the fourth for the Achill Bible and Church Missionary Society, and the fifth for donations of clothing; a sixth – may be occasional – for relief of distress in Achill and the seventh, may be for the Infant School. From all these sources a large sum is collected and this sum seems to be expended on salaries for missionaries, schoolmasters and schoolmistresses, workmen's wages, repairs, buildings, expenses of printing office, dispensary, etc. – the affairs of the Mission being administered by a committee of gentlemen of irreproachable character, the greater number of whom probably have never visited the settlement, but who believe that it is really conferring a practical benefit on the community.[62]

The report for the year 1835, included an abstract of the cash account, income and expenditure, for that year. This was certified by Robert Daly and W. H. Porter as auditors. There was also a record of the cash received by Edward Nangle up to 20 April 1836 and the cash expended from this account. Nangle appended a note

> this account contains an acknowledgement of money, entrusted to my stewardship only; any sums which passed through my hands and are not mentioned here, will be acknowledged in the report of the committee. I must here express our obligation to several friends in Dublin, for valuable donations of medicine; and Dr Adams also desires to acknowledge the aid received from the House of Industry for persons afflicted with hernia.[63]

This report continued with long lists of names and amounts of money, either subscribed or donated by persons in both England and Ireland. Sometimes the amounts given were for specific purposes, e.g., for reclaiming land to annex to the cottages on the Protestant settlement in Achill (collected by Mrs Reynell, Cheltenham − £16); another was for the Refuge, and yet another for the building of a church (£50 was given by an 'unknown friend'). Some appear to have been in the form of an annual subscription while others were collected following sermons preached by Edward Nangle and other clergy in both England and Ireland.[64] Some idea of the amounts received in subscriptions, donations and collections can be seen from the details set out in appendix 2.

The funds contributed for the purchase of the Achill estate in 1851 amounted to some £10,500, details of which are contained in the *17th Report*. For this fund, there was one anonymous contribution of £300. Others included eight at £100 each; 323 subscribing sums of between £4 and £60; sixty-five gave £10 each and 185 gave £5 each. In addition, 1,709 persons subscribed sums ranging from 4*d.* from a little boy, Master Fairfield 6*d.*, and others from 1s. up to £4. In addition to lists of individual subscribers, a total of 873 collections were set out showing amounts collected ranging from as low as 5*s.* 6*d.* to as high as £249. 15*s.* 7*d.*, this latter sum was described as the 'Earl of Enniskillen's collection' which was made up of twenty-three separate collections. Some collections were identified as coming from the Liverpool and the Norwich Protestant associations. There was also a Manchester branch association for the Achill Mission.[65]

It is not always clear from the accounts whether the moneys received for specific purposes were used for those purposes, or whether they went into a general account from which expenditure for the administration of the Mission was drawn. However, they do reveal the type of expenditure incurred by the Mission. Had all of the annual reports and accounts survived, it would have been possible to provide more detailed information about the on-going development of the Mission, especially in the early years.

The Achill Mission was largely dependant on voluntary subscriptions without which it could not have survived for as long as it did, and when these declined, following the purchase of the Achill estate in 1851, the Mission almost totally collapsed. While the names of donors were supplied, unfortunately, few addresses were given. However, it is generally believed that most of the money subscribed came from England. The *Achill Herald* was distributed widely in many countries of the world, including Canada and India, and appeals for funds, published in its pages, therefore, had a wide circulation. Accounts of outrages against the Mission and religious controversy ensured an increase in contributions.

Edward Nangle, sometimes accompanied by another, was indefatigable in his efforts to raise funds for the Mission in both England and Ireland, and this was mainly achieved by preaching sermons which were followed by collections. He was frequently away from Achill on such visits, once for a period of three months with Charles Seymour, rector of Achill parish, when they endeavoured to raise funds for the importation of a cargo of grain for which Nangle had made himself personally responsible.[66] Writing to his wife from Amersham in England in January 1838, he referred to a number of other visits in the vicinity. He stated that in no instances had he asked for money, but 'merely laid my case before Christian friends, and I have already received £250, besides the £2,400 for the churches and clergymen's houses at Dugort and Inishbegil.' He continued

> I mean to leave London on the 14th. I purpose to visit Ashby, Birmingham, and Wolverhampton on my way to Liverpool, so I expect to reach home about the 1st of February. I think I shall have to come to England again in May, when I can visit Exeter, Bath, Clifton, Oxford, Cambridge, Hereford, and Chester.[67]

Other places mentioned on his proposed itinerary were Clevedon, Cheltenham, Sheffield, Reading, Altringham, Kendal, Stafford and Manchester.[68]

Reports of physical attacks and threats against persons attached to the Mission, as well as adverse written reports, often giving the impression of a beleaguered institution, frequently generated a very large inflow of funds. A recurring theme throughout the early years of the settlement was the constant confrontation between the missionaries and their followers and the Catholic clergy and the people of the island. Initially, there appears to have been friendly relations between the local people and the newcomers. However, when schools were opened and Catholic children began to be taught in those run by the Mission, the Catholic clergy quickly realised that this was a serious threat to their authority and they opposed them with vigour. A system of 'exclusive dealing' was introduced which had serious consequences for the Mission. The local people were forbidden to work for the settlement or to supply it with goods, and parents were told not to send their children to the Mission schools. It was alleged by Nangle, no doubt with some truth, that those who defied these prohibitions were 'cursed from the altar.' One such incident, alleged to have taken place, concerned a priest, Patrick Harley, who was sent to Achill to prepare for a visit by Dr MacHale, Catholic archbishop of Tuam, in September 1838. The priest was reported to have publicly cursed from the altar several named persons from the settlement, and at the same time forbade people to speak to them or have any dealings with them.[69]

An example of exclusive dealing occured when a man, who, grateful for the free treatment he had received for a painful complaint, promised to sell some potatoes to Dr Adams, but they never arrived. The man later explained that the priest would not allow him to sell the potatoes to Dr Adams.[70] According to Nangle, 'an attempt was made to starve us out of the island by the rigid enforcement of a system of exclusive dealing which was renewed under the episcopal sanction of Dr MacHale when he visited the island in 1838.'[71] Exclusive dealing meant that the Mission had to import goods and supplies from Westport at a much higher cost than had they been able to obtain them locally. They also had to bring in labourers and other workers to assist with the reclaiming of land, the sowing of crops and the building of houses. There were also reports of assaults, damage to property, and the intimidation of those Catholics who wished to stay at the Mission.

At a very early stage of the development of the Mission, the opposition of the Catholic clergy became apparent. In 1837, Nangle noted that 'a furious persecution was got up by the Roman Catholic priests and Dr MacHale, who aimed at nothing short of the expulsion of the missionaries from the island.'[72] Dr MacHale 'visited Achill in the autumn of 1835 and gave full effect to the maledictions and the threats of the priests who had been sent to prepare the way before him'.[73] According to Seddall, the opposition which Nangle encountered came from the priests rather than the people.[74]

There were allegations of assaults recorded as early as October 1835 when Thomas Bulfin, of the constabulary office in Castlebar, wrote to Major Warburton, the inspector general of police, about an assault on one of the scripture readers from the Mission. A complaint was made by John Gardiner, returning to Achill after attending the Quarter Sessions in Castlebar which had dealt with a previous assault claim of his. Gardiner, on being asked if he was a Bible reader replied in the affirmative. He was then assaulted by one John Levingston who kicked him in the thigh and gave him a blow with his clenched fist to the side of the head.[75] It will be recalled that Gardiner was one of the two scripture readers named by Mrs Adams. This assault was fairly typical of other assaults perpetrated against persons associated with the Mission. Scripture readers appear to have been a particular target for assault. There were reports of a number of assaults against Rev. Baylee and the scripture readers who accompanied him. It appears that Baylee was severely beaten on one occasion. A heavy cudgel with an iron ferule at the end of it was used in the assault inflicting a deep wound on his forehead which left a permanent mark.[76]

In August 1837, Baylee travelled to Clare Island attempting to establish a mission station there. Because of threats to cut the sails of his boat, the boatman who had brought him to the island sailed away without him. Baylee was rescued by the constable in charge of Clare island who had just returned to the island and had seen the boat sail away. The constable sent a sub-constable and a coastguard to protect Baylee and escort him to the lighthouse two miles away. They were shouted at on the way, and Baylee was detained on the island next day because the priest ordered that he should not get a boat.[77] There was another incident during the visit of the bishop, presumably Dr MacHale, to Clare island when two schoolmasters and a scripture reader were assaulted.[78]

The year 1837 seems to have been full of such incidents relating to Achill. In February, the chief constable, Fergus Ferrall, in a report citing other incidents, wrote that

> The Chief Constable begs to say he finds it remarkably unpleasant to act between these conflicting parties who declaim each in their time so loudly against the police one for giving, and the other for refusing and he begs to add he shall endeavour to act as disinterested a part as he possibly can between the belligerents while their animosity continues.[79]

In July the same year, there was a report that Rev. Martin Connolly, parish priest of Achill and his assistant Rev. William Roach, proceeded to Bullsmouth, entered Rev. Baylee's schoolhouse and took the books from the children, beat them and turned them out of the schoolhouse and threatened the schoolmaster.[80]

These are but a few examples of intimidation which occurred following the establishment of the missionary settlement. There were complaints about shouting and the hurling of verbal abuse at people from the Mission. The throwing of stones and the possible threat to use or the actual use of a whip were also reported. There were complaints that boats belonging to the Mission were damaged, and on other occasions that windows in houses were broken. One such complaint was made by Nangle on 5 March, 1839, when he referred to stones being thrown at Henry McLoughlin's window and breaking two panes of glass, a quart bottle and shattering part of the sash, and also that a pane of glass was broken in Neal Grealis's window. Both of these men were employed at the colony. A reward of £20 was offered for information (fig. 4).[81] It has to be said that these threats were believed by Nangle and his associates to have been orchestrated by the Catholic clergy. While this may have been so, there were frequent incidences of provocation on the part of those associated with the Mission.

£20
REWARD.

I HEREBY Offer a REWARD of

TWENTY POUNDS

To any Person who shall, within six
months from the date hereof, give me
such information as may enable me to
discover and bring to Justice all
or any of the Persons who were con-
cerened in assaulting the Dwellings,
on the night of the 3rd instant, of
Henry M'Loughiln and *Neal Grealis*, on the lands of *Doogarth*, in the
Island of *Achill*, by throwing stones
through their Windows.

F. FERRALL,
Chief Constable.

Newport-pratt. 12th March. 1839.

4. '£20 Reward', issued by the Chief Constable, Newport-Pratt, 1839.
(Source: NAI, Outrage papers, Mayo)

One of the outrage reports relating to the maiming of cattle belonging to
Francis Reynolds, a civilian coastguard, in September 1838, commented that
– 'the gentleman is much disliked because he has been active in suppressing
illicit distillation in the island of Achill to which I attribute the attack now
made on his property.'[82] On 14 December that year, it was reported that
Reynolds was involved in a row over an alleged theft from a wreck and was

struck with a spade which fractured his skull. He died later from his injuries. A couple from Keel, John and Bridget Lavelle, were arrested and charged with the offence but were later acquitted on the grounds of self-defence.[83] Another version tells of Reynold's pursuit of a group of assailants who had been pelting him with stones. He followed them into the house where he received the wound which proved fatal.[84] Reynolds left a wife and eight children. A special fund was set up by the Mission for the education of the children and subscriptions received were regularly listed in the *Achill Herald*.[85]

By the late 1830s, in spite of opposition, Nangle had established a missionary settlement with both an administrative and physical structure in which people could live and work. The administrative structure was comprised of a Dublin committee, which issued *Annual Reports* and accounts and ensured continuity over time, and a local committee which dealt with the day to day running of the missionary settlement.

Evolution of the settlement 1833–45

Having secured a lease of 130 acres of mountainy Achill land, a steward was appointed in the summer of 1833 to superintend the reclamation of the land and to oversee the building of some houses. Most of the materials for the first of the buildings were brought by boat to the strand below Dugort in 1833. When Edward Nangle arrived with his family in 1834, a farm had been enclosed and two houses erected for the accommodation of two families. By 1835, a range of buildings had been constructed for persons connected with the work of the Mission. The honorary physician to the Mission, Dr Neason Adams, had a house built for himself and his wife at his own expense on a strip of land given to him by the committee. They arrived on Achill on 18 December 1835.[1]

A church, capable of accommodating about 140 persons was found necessary because of an increase in the congregation. In addition, eight cottages were built to accommodate those families who had placed themselves and their children under spiritual instruction at the Mission.[2] A further eight cottages were being built and these were intended for tenants. Eighteen families (all, with exception of one, converts from Catholicism) required accommodation and in order to provide for such a number of persons who had sought protection from the priests, two lots of land and two houses in the immediate neighbourhood of the settlement were purchased for a modest sum.[3] In the accounts for 1835, it was noted that £4. 8s. 0d. was paid for a holding in Dugort while £30 was spent on cottages and reclaiming land.[4] The houses were intended to accommodate two families who would pay a rent for their holdings which would save the Mission from any financial loss. These were afterwards referred to as the 'Refuge'. Also in the same year, £1,128. 2s. 11d. was spent on 'sundries in the island of Achill', which included erecting the church and other buildings, tillage, salary to missionaries, scripture readers, steward, etc. Unfortunately, this figure was not broken down and it is not possible to determine how much was spent on the buildings.[5]

In spite of the very inclement weather in the spring of 1835, with almost incessant storms, heavy snow and rain, the Mission expected to have some twenty-six acres of reclaimed land brought into use in addition to those previously cultivated.[6] Field labour, such as the sowing of crops, was the main pre-occupation at this time. But there were a number of factors working against the settlement. The peasantry were forbidden by the priests to work for the Mission in helping to sow crops with awful threats against those who defied this prohibition. They were also ordered not to sell provisions to anyone belonging to the Mission. It was alleged that the priests had even sent a messenger to the opposite coast to ensure the cutting off of the supply of sea-wrack which was needed to manure the land.[7] It was also said that the priest published a letter in the Dublin newspapers in an effort to cut off the supply of funds by representing the work of the Mission as unworthy of the support of the Christian public. However, this was counteracted by the placing of an advertisement by the Mission in a London newspaper which was followed by an inflow of funds. Provisions were imported from the mainland and labourers were brought from Westport to carry out the spring sowing.[8]

Having dealt with the sowing of crops, it was the intention at this time to seek to improve the habits of the poor people resident on the Mission's lands by enforcing cleanliness and encouraging domestic industry among the women and children. With a view to the latter, the intention was to introduce the manufacture of coarse linen and cloth, and the knitting of stockings. A weaver was brought in and settled in one of the cottages. The sowing of flax was another project. One of the industries introduced into his estates at Newport by Sir Richard O'Donnel, was the sowing of flax and this may have influenced Nangle to follow his example. The wool for the coarse cloth and stockings had to be purchased in Westport or Castlebar. The coarse linen cloth was for home consumption and it was hoped to find a market for the stockings in Dublin.[9] From these details, it can be seen that efforts were being made to introduce a work ethic into the area and to endeavour to create a village which was quite unlike that of any other village settlement on the island at that time.

By 1838, a corn mill with a kiln for drying the corn and a tuck mill for thickening frieze had been built, the former used not only for disposing of the grain grown on the farm by converting it into meal but also converting oats purchased in Westport into meal and thereby gaining an income for the Mission. The return from the mill and farm between 1 October and 31 December 1839 was given as £127.[10] It appears that a lease for ever was obtained from Sir Richard O'Donnel for the site on which the two mills were located. It was expected that the two mills would cost upwards of £200 and about £40 had been received by the time the building commenced.[11] However, in October of that year, Nangle listed the names of subscribers to a fund for the erection of the mills, stating that the amount received (about £99) fell far short of what was needed.[12] It is interesting to note that this was not the only example of planning and building on the part of the Mission, before there were sufficient funds to complete the project.

A shop had also been established at the settlement for the sale of such articles of clothing 'as are used by the peasantry', and the stock had been enlarged. It was even contemplated freighting a small vessel at Liverpool to convey goods imported directly from the manufacturers and which could be sold 'at such a low rate as would ensure the custom of the whole island.'[13] However, it is not certain that this plan was followed through.

Another development was the opening of a small hotel at the settlement in the spring of 1839 for the accommodation of visitors to the Mission.[14] In the *Report* covering the year 1839, Nangle recorded that 'we had upwards of one hundred visitors last spring and summer.'[15] Many attribute the development of the tourist industry in Achill to the establishment of this hotel. Publicity about the Mission and curiosity aroused by its controversial reputation certainly brought many visitors to Dugort. Additional buildings erected about this time were four small slated houses on the plot of ground on which the mill stood. Also a small infirmary for the children of the place was in the course of being built. Other improvements were the completion of a road through the bog and farm, the fencing off of four acres of land and the reclamation of twelve acres of land around the settlement for planting that spring (1840).[16]

The 'Achill orphan refuge', also described as the 'orphan asylum', was instituted in March 1838, for the education of the orphan children of Roman Catholic parents, as Protestants. Four comfortable cottages, each capable of containing twenty-five children, with a married couple to supervise them, were built.[17] The cost of building a cottage was given as £10, and £40 was paid on account for the building of a dining hall and store.[18]

Plans for the colonisation of the island of Inishbiggle (637 acres), which had been leased from Sir Richard O'Donnel in 1837, were in progress by 1839. Two families had built their houses on Inishbiggle and had reclaimed five acres of land which was ready for sowing the following spring (1840).[19] A few years later, the townland of Mweelin, which lies about five miles from Dugort in south-west Achill, containing 1,444 acres, came under Mission management and became the location of a subsidiary missionary settlement. It consisted of a linear village of twelve cottages, a schoolhouse, a minister's residence, a training school for teachers and scripture readers and a small church, all of which had been built by 1850. But it never attracted the same attention from visitors, probably because it was off the beaten track, or the same notoriety as the colony itself.[20]

There were plans for a parish church and glebe house to be built on Achill. Also, an application had been made through the rector of the parish to the bishop for his consent for the building of a church at the settlement under a recent act of parliament which would connect them regularly with the Established Church, and bring them under episcopal jurisdiction while leaving appointments in the hands of the trustees. The building of a church along the same lines was envisaged for Inishbiggle where there was a growing congregation.[21] In respect of funding, Nangle reported that an individual with generosity 'supplies funds for the erection of the two churches and two ministers' houses connected with them'.[22] It appears that the sum of £2,400 mentioned in the first chapter relates to this report. But the Church of St Thomas in Dugort was not built until after the Famine.

Yet another development was of a 'house of recovery', which consisted of nurse-tenders' apartments, a bathroom, and two rooms for convalescent patients; overhead a store room, and three rooms for those suffering from contagious diseases. This building was expected to be roofed by the following March.[23] Expenditure on the project included £37 paid to the builder. A sum of £5. 16s. 8d. was paid on account to the carpenter, nailer and slater, while the six tons of slates cost £19. 10s. 0d., and, for boat and landing (presumably for transporting the slates), the cost was £4. 5s. 0d., making a total of £66. 11s. 8d. It was noted that 'a FEW subscribers are wanted to finish this necessary undertaking'.[24] This was another example of a building being proceeded with before all the necessary funding was in place.

An appeal for funds for relief of distress in Achill was made by the Mission following a failure of the potato crop in 1838 and this was used to improve the infrastructure of the settlement. The money received was spent in strict accordance with the statement issued with the appeal and no gratuitous relief was given except where persons were incapable of working. This distress fund was used to carry out the following works:–

1. An excellent cart road, twenty-one feet wide and about half an English mile was made through the Mission land, besides giving access to the turf bog, afforded great facility for reclaiming the best part of their farm.
2. About one hundred perches of road was repaired through the farm and island.
3. Twelve English acres of land were reclaimed.
4. A few hundred of perches of drains were laid.
5. Upwards of one hundred perches of fences were made.
6. One small bridge was erected over the tail race of their mill and four gullets were built.
7. The cottages on the settlement were repaired and the mill dam secured by a permanent embankment.

Besides the people belonging to the settlement, daily employment on these works was also given to about 140 of the local population, which meant that the Mission did not have to bring in labourers from other parts of the country. This may have been an indication of better relations with their neighbours. The total amount received for the distress fund was £436. 19s. 7d., and the amount paid to labourers and for the relief of the poor was £406. 14s. 4d., leaving a balance of £30. 5s. 3d.[25] It is worth noting here that all of the works mentioned were for the benefit of the Mission.

The year 1842 saw the completion of a large building, containing the orphan dining-hall, kitchen, stores, and two large schoolrooms. This building was destroyed by an accidental fire in February 1843. The building itself, as well as the goods in store, were insured to the full amount of their value so that no loss was sustained, other than the temporary inconvenience pending the repair of the building, and the schoolroom furniture which was not insured.[26]

During the previous year, a range of offices was built at the rear of Nangle's house, and a substantial slated house containing apartments for the school-master and an airy dormitory for twenty-five orphan boys was also erected at the settlement. Another cottage was built, and a small cow-house was added to each of the cottages previously erected (fourteen cow-houses in all). The farm, which was purchased, had been transferred to the orphans, and the return from it answered expectations.[27] A sum of £318. 6s. 2d. was spent on buildings in 1842, £28. 17s. 9d. on farming implements and jaunting car, £4. 8s. 6d. on boats and £3. 4s. 8d. for a tuck mill on Inishbiggle.[28] In the same year, £4. 6s. was spent building out-offices at the hospital, and £2 was spent for painting and glazing at the hospital.[29]

One of the significant events of the year 1835 was the arrival of the printing press on which the *Achill Herald*, or to give it is full title *The Achill Missionary Herald and Western Witness*, was printed. The *Achill Herald* was to play an important part in the progress and survival of the Mission. Writing in 1865, Nangle recalled the arrival of the printing press

> In this stage of my narrative, I must notice an event of very great importance and which contributed, in no small degree to the success of the Achill Mission – the establishment of a printing office in our infant settlement. The following extract from my journal, dated December, 1835, alludes to this event:–
>
> Tuesday – The hooker, with our printing press on board, came into the bay. It blew so hard that we could not load the cargo. The men on board the boat had much difficulty in mooring her: having secured her as best they could, they took to the small boat, and at the peril of their lives made for the shore, leaving the hooker to the mercy of the wind and the waves. We expected that she would have broken from her moorings; however, her cable held fast, and towards evening the gale subsided, so that they were able to bring her out of the bay into the harbour.
>
> A few days after the boat again came into the bay, and her cargo was safely landed, it was an interesting sight to see the children of some of the converts carry the lighter parts of the printing press up to the settlement, where they were to be used for emancipating others from the ignorance and bondage from which they had been delivered. We are indebted for this gift to some friends in London and York. We believe that the great day of final account alone will disclose the amount of good accomplished by its instrumentality.[30]

Although the printing press arrived in December 1835, it was not until two and a half years later that the first issue of the *Achill Herald* appeared (12 July 1837). It is not clear why there should have been such a delay. Kenneth McNally writing in his book on Achill (1973) states that

> no details of the press itself have been preserved in any correspondence relating to the administration of the Achill Missionary Estate. There are no receipts for its purchase, probably because it was a gift from supporters in London and York. In addition to English typefaces, Irish, Greek and Hebrew fonts were in regular use. Experienced printers were employed, including William Pugh and George Bozman, though it was said that Mr Nangle was himself competent in typesetting procedures.[31]

There is a record of the marriage of William Pugh and Frances Flanagan, both of Achill Parish, on 6 December 1838 when the ceremony was performed by Rev. Edward Nangle.[32] There is also a record of the baptism of a son (Charles John) of William Pugh (a printer) and his wife Frances in October 1839.[33] There is no record of when William Pugh arrived in Achill or where he came from but since the marriage record shows that he was 'of the parish of Achill' at the time of his marriage in 1838, it may be assumed that he was the first printer employed there. There is a record in the register of baptisms of a daughter born to George and Martha Awe in 1844.[34] He was described as a printer. Kenneth McNally also refers to George Bozman. There is no reference to George Bozman in the registers of baptisms, marriages or burials, but there are a number of references to him in the Cancelled Books in the Valuation Office (in 1855 and also in 1859). George Awe is also mentioned in the Cancelled Books.[35]

The printing office, which was growing in efficiency, was under the supervision of an experienced printer assisted by five apprentices, four of them orphans who were educated at the settlement. The output from this office included thousands of sheets of printing for the immediate use of the settlement, 2,000 copies of *The Confessions of a French Priest* containing two hundred and forty pages, 5,000 copies of two sermons in reply to the address of the Hon. and Rev. George Spencer, and 1,000 copies of the correspondence with Mr S.C. Hall, as well as many other items. A reprint of Neilson's *Irish Grammar* was also undertaken. With regard to the latter item, it was noted that this would have been completed at an earlier date but for the fact that a font of Irish type, which had been ordered, was stolen from the carrier to whom it was entrusted. In 1841, an appeal was made to friends of the Mission, who had printing requirements for circulars, tracts, pamphlets or books, to place their orders with the Mission and the work, when finished, would be sent by mail to any part of Dublin without any charge for carriage. It was hoped that this would help the Mission to become as independent as possible of voluntary support.[36]

In addition to the previously mentioned activities, the printing office was also responsible for the printing of 2,000 copies of the *Achill Herald*. It consisted of twelve closely printed medium quarto pages and was published monthly at a cost of 5s. per annum, payable in advance.[37] The original subscription was 4s. per annum but the cost was increased in 1841. The reason given by Nangle for the increase was 'the remoteness of the locality from the civilized part of the country occasions expenses of which persons in more favourable circumstances can form no conception. For a considerable time, if so much as a screw of the press went out of order, we were obliged to send it twenty-five to thirty-one miles to be repaired.' He added that

> there are various other financial details with which we need not trouble our readers, what we have said may suffice to show them that our paper could not be conducted on a lower rate of subscription without a forfeiture on the part of the proprietor of the moderate remuneration which he has a right to expect in return for the capital sunk and the time expended in the establishment and conduct of his paper.[38]

It appears that Nangle found that he could support and educate his family by the publication of the *Achill Herald* and by the sale of his books, hence the reference to his proprietorship of the paper in the above quotation. He gave up a salary of £150 a year which he received from the Dublin committee.[39]

There were two major issues facing the Mission in 1842. One was the lack of sufficient accommodation for the Mission's settlers and the inability of their landlord to give them a lease in perpetuity which deterred them from spending any more money on expanding the settlement. The local committee suggested that a large tract of reclaimable land should be taken on a lease forever in some other part of the country. It was believed that the experience acquired in the management of the experiment in Achill would enable them to establish another similar settlement elsewhere with confidence. The second issue concerned the young people who were educated by the Mission and were now approaching manhood. It was felt that these young men might be established to their advantage, and that of the cause, in a new settlement. This was not to say that the local committee intended abandoning the Achill Mission at Dugort, far from it. But the Mission's lands were only held on a lease of 'three lives or thirty-one years'. While the landlord had pledged to renew the lease of 130 acres on which the settlement stood as often as required during his lifetime, without any increase in rent, there was an element of uncertainty about the future. The three acres on which the mill stood were held under an act of parliament which gave enlarged leasing power to tenants for life or a lease of lives renewable for ever, for the sites of mills.[40]

Notwithstanding the concern expressed by the local committee about their lease, building works continued during the next two years. In 1843, the restoration commenced of the large building containing schoolrooms, stores, the orphan dining-hall and kitchen which had been destroyed by an accidental fire in February of that year. The Royal Exchange Insurance Company, without any hesitation, re-imbursed the Mission on the basis of the estimated amount of the damage. However, the restoration of the building cost much more as it was made two feet higher than the previous building, and a new kitchen and other offices were added to it.[41]

A number of improvements were carried out in the year 1844. The walls of two houses, each containing eight rooms, with a kitchen and pantry were built. A room was added to each of the houses of the steward and the printer. Two two-roomed cottages were finished and another was being built. A stable and loft, covered with a slate roof, were added to the house rented from the Mission by the coastguard officer. A slated cow-house was added to the hospital, and the offices connected with the orphan dining-hall and dwelling house were also slated. The printing office, which had been partially destroyed by an accidental fire, was re-built on a new and improved plan. It now measured forty feet long by eighteen feet wide, with a good slated roof and boarded floor. The costs obtained from the insurers for this re-building did not include the cost of the timber and carpenter's tools which were lost in the fire. A forge was set up in the room where the tuck-mill formerly stood. Also a farmhouse at Mweelin had been roofed.[42] In that year also, a fund was set up to provide a house for the use of priests who had converted to Protestantism, and one individual undertook the expense of building a spacious hotel which was expected to be ready in May 1845.[43]

It will be recalled that access to the island and within the island was always difficult with its poor roads and lack of transport. A direct result of the presence of the missionary settlement was the opening of the post office in Dugort leading to better communications. In the early days of the Mission, post boys were employed to convey mail, and especially copies of the *Achill Herald*, to the outside world, and there were a number of reports of post boys being attacked and threatened. As detailed in the accounts to the end of December 1842, the cost of postage and a postman was £35. 12s. 10d.[44] Up to that time the cost of conveying letters and parcels amounted to £20 per annum. The next improvement was the commencement of a mail car service between Dugort and Newport at a cost of £80 (including the cost of the car). Income from the carriage of parcels and passengers together with an allowance of £20 from the Post Office for the carriage of mail came to within £10 of clearing the daily costs. The Mission achieved a saving of £10 on an outlay of £70. They reckoned that, with an expected influx of English travellers, there would be a profit for the Mission.[45] A contract for the conveyance of mail had been taken by the settlement, although it was stated the sum allowed by the post office was a very inadequate remuneration. Mail was conveyed to and from Newport regularly, three times weekly, Tuesday,

5. Dugort and Slievemore mountain. The missionary settlement
and Achill mailcar, *c.*1850. (Source: RCBL).

Thursdays and Saturday, by a 'well-appointed mail car which also carried four passengers'. It was expected that the money received for conveyance of passengers and parcels would save the settlement from loss. According to an advertisement in January 1844, the Achill mail left from the post office in Dugort at 11.15 am and arrived at the Sound at 1.15 p.m. and on the return left the Sound at 1 p.m. arriving at Dugort at 4 p.m. The fares were Dugort to Achill Sound 1s., Dugort to Mulranny 2s. 6d., and Dugort to Newport 3s. 6d. This arrangement made access to and from the settlement much easier as passengers could connect with transport to places farther afield.[46]

The expansion of the physical fabric of the settlement was accompanied by a steady growth in its population. In the absence of comprehensive records of the people who lived in the Achill missionary settlement, a census of population can only be derived from the sources which have survived. According to the religious census of 1834, referred to in the introduction, there were only seventy-six Protestants, mostly coast guardsmen, their families and some other officials, resident in the whole of Achill.[47]

The first person associated with the missionary settlement was the steward who was appointed in 1833 by the Dublin committee. It appears that he was originally a Roman Catholic but through contact with the Irish Society studied the scriptures through the medium of Irish and successively filled the positions of pupil-teacher and inspector. He also learned to read and write in English and to keep accounts. According to Nangle, he held the position of steward for several years before going to Glasgow.[48] But this was possibly only for two years as Charles Bridger in his evidence given, in April 1837, to the Select Committee of the House of Lords appointed to enquire into the progress and operation of the new plan for education in Ireland, stated that he had been land steward at the settlement 'since August twelvemonth', (1835).[49] Bridger, a Protestant from the south of England, was in Ireland for ten to eleven years before being employed by the Dublin committee of the Achill Mission at a salary of £40 per annum. In 1834, Edward Nangle arrived with his wife and presumably their three children who were born outside Achill, two in Dublin in 1830 and 1831 and the third who was born in Ballina in 1833. They were soon joined by an assistant to Nangle, Rev. Joseph Duncan, two scripture readers named Joyce and Gardiner, and Alexander Lendrum and his six children. From the description of their living conditions given by Mrs Adams, wife of Dr Neason Adams, in about 1836, two of the available rooms had been converted into a printing office, the two scripture readers, Gardiner and Joyce and the Lendrum family were all accommodated there at that time.[50] It is also likely that the printer, William Pugh, lived there too from 1835 or 1836 onwards.

In 1842, Nangle gave the population of the settlement as

Total number of families	64	individuals	311
Families originally Protestant	13	individuals	56
Families originally Catholic	51	individuals	255
Orphan children of Roman Catholic parents	100		
Orphans apprenticed in the Colony	9		

Accompanying these figures was the following explanation

> of the Romish families above enumerated, thirty, containing one hundred and fifty-five individuals, were brought over by the immediate instrumentality of the Mission, and of these, twenty-seven families, including one hundred and thirty-five individuals were natives of Achill, or the surrounding district. Several families and individuals, who were brought out of popery by the instrumentality of the Mission, and who are now living in different parts of England, Ireland and America, are not included in the above enumeration; neither have we included twelve originally Protestant families, who, though belonging to the congregation, do not reside in the settlement. The Mission has now the spiritual charge of nearly 500 souls.[51]

In the year 1843, Nangle claimed there were

Families originally Protestant	46	individuals	185
Families originally Catholic	59	individuals	270
Totals	105		455[52]

From the above figures, it can be seen that the number of Protestant families at the settlement increased from thirteen in 1842 to forty-six families by 1843. During the same period, the number of families, originally Catholic, increased from fifty-one to fifty-nine of the total number of families. Clearly, there was a greater increase in the number of families who were originally Protestant attached to the settlement than in the number of families who were originally Catholics. There is no clear explanation for the increase in the number of Protestant families, described as being natives of Achill and the surrounding district, from thirteen in 1842 to forty-six in 1843. It is possible that people who were brought in from Newport and Westport, because of the exclusive dealing prohibition, might have been described as coming from a surrounding district. The number of Roman Catholic families increased by eight (fifteen persons) compared with an increase of thirty-three Protestant families (129 persons) in the two years.' It would appear, therefore, that the total population of the settlement increased by 144 between 1842 and 1843. Such a large growth can only be explained by immigration into the settlement as Protestants from outside seem to have been placed there.

It is worth noting here, that in the census of 1841, the population of Dugort was given as 319 (157 males and 162 females), and one may assume that the missionary settlement was counted within the area described as Dugort.[53] If the figure of 319 is compared with the figures given by the Mission for the year 1842 as set out above, the population of the settlement was 420 (including those who were originally Protestant or Catholics plus the orphans), thereby showing an increase of 101 in one year or at most a year and a half.

The first census of the population of Ireland which gave separate figures for the townlands of Dugort was that of 1841. The three areas or townlands were Dugort, Dugort East and Dugort West. These divisions were also used by the Ordnance Survey and in Griffith's Valuation of Tenements as well as in the 1841 census and subsequent censuses. The 1841 census only provided a breakdown of figures on the basis of the three areas (table 1). Griffith, on the other hand, indicated the names of owners and lessors of land and property, with separate lists for the settlement and Rock Lane, but not the numbers in each household.[54]

Some of those who were counted under Dugort East and Dugort West may have been included in the Mission's figures, but without accurate information, the reliability of the population figures given by the Mission is open to question. However, if we assume that the census figures as given for

Table 1. Population of Dugort townlands

Townland	1841				1851		
	Male	Female	Total		Male	Female	Total
Dugort	157	162	319		215	236	451
Dugort East	21	17	38		14	15	29
Dugort West	183	165	348		116	122	238

Source: Census 1841 and census 1851.[55]

Dugort equate with those of the settlement, it is possible to take the census figures as accurate ones for the settlement.

Something of the nature of the pre-Famine population change can be seen in the parish registers. Although these registers were begun in the late 1830s, with the passage of time many of the entries have either completely faded or the writing has deteriorated to such an extent as to make them difficult to decipher. Another problem with the registers is that in the case of the register of baptisms, some records are incomplete, some have the same number assigned to more than one record, some have no number and some records are out of year sequence. Despite these deficiencies, the register of baptisms provides, in most cases, details of the date of baptism, child's christian name, the christian and surnames of the parents, their abode at the time of the baptism, the quality, trade or profession of the father and by whom the ceremony was performed. There was also a date of birth column which was rarely completed, but where it was filled in it could be used either for cross-referencing with the date of the baptism or instead of the date of baptism if the latter was missing. An examination of the baptisms performed in Dugort from 1838 to 1845 inclusive, shows that there were more males than females baptised (table 2). The figures have been broken down into three categories, Colony/Dugort, outside the colony and unclear records. Male and female figures are given for the first two.[56]

Table 2. Baptisms in Achill parish: 1838–45

	Colony/Dugort	Outside Colony	Unclear	Total
Male	49	27		
Female	33	22		
Totals	82	49	10	141

Source: Parish registers.[57]

The number of baptisms compared with those of burials demonstrates the vitality of the population growth (table 3).

Table 3. Burials in Achill parish, 1838–45

	Colony/ Dugort	Outside Colony	Orphan Colony	Total
Male	13	1	6	20
Female	6	1	2	9
Totals	19	2	8	29

Source: Parish registers.[58]

Apart from two males aged fifty and fifty-two, the ages, when given, ranged from one to sixteen years. In the case of females, only two ages were given (four and twelve years respectively). Six of the male orphans who died during this period were between the ages of five and nine years, but no ages were given for the two females. A possible explanation is that there were frequent bouts of illness in the colony as well as in the island as a whole which appear to have affected the death rate in the younger age group rather than in older people.

There was a total of nineteen male and eight female burials in the combined colony and orphan colony. Between 1838 and 1845, there were twenty more baptisms of males over burials, and twenty-five more baptisms of females over burials. The total number baptisms was eighty-two and the total number of burials for the same period was twenty-seven, an increase of fifty-five baptisms over burials. All this suggests a vigorous growth in population. This may be linked to rapid inflow of population as a result of immigration.

Table 4. Marriages in Achill parish, 1838–45

Year	Number	Number of marriages per month
1838	7	January (2); February (1); March (1); December (3)
1839	2	March (1); November (1)
1840	1	June (1)
1841	0	No marriages recorded
1842	4	January (1); query 1); September (1); November (1)
1843	6	April (1); August (1); Oct. (1); Nov. (2); Dec. (1)
1844	7	February (2); March (1); June (1); July (3)
1845	2	March (2).
Total	29	

Source: Parish register.[59]

As can be seen from table 4, while there was no well-defined pattern as to the month in which couples married, most marriages took place in the early and late months of the year, suggesting that couples were needed during the April to August period for farm and other work. Only one marriage of the twenty-nine was recorded as being by licence and that was in 1842. Achill was given by all but one as the place of residence at the time of marriage – the other one gave Ballycroy. There is no way of knowing from which part of Achill the couples came. The officiating clergyman for all but two of the marriages was Edward Nangle, Edward Lowe having performed the other two.[60]

The rapidly growing population had to be provided with work, and food was required to feed them, so a priority was the development of agriculture. The dominance of agriculture in the economy of the settlement is clear from the trades or occupations of the fathers as given in the baptismal register entries between 1838–45.

Table 5. Principal occupations of fathers, 1838–45

Year	Labourers	Others	Totals
1838	8	7	15
1839	9	8	17
1840	5	14	19
1841	11	5	16
1842	5	10	15
1843	8	9	17
1844	8	13	21
1845	12	8	20
Totals	66	74	140

Source: Achill parish baptismal register.[61]

The provision of agricultural produce was essential for the viability of the settlement and the hope was that it would render it independent of outside assistance. As can be seen from table 5, the most numerous occupation was that of labourer. Of the other seventy-four, thirty-eight gave 'coastguard' as their occupation. Other trades and professions included were carpenter, printer, clerk, teacher, slater, mason, tailor, steward, scripture reader, policeman, Achill Mission agent. A comparable breakdown from the marriage registers was not possible as the more detailed register did not begin until 1845.

Also in most of the issues of the *Achill Herald*, there are reports of the 'weather and the crops' which were sometimes included under 'local and provincial news.' From these reports it is possible to trace the weather and its effects on farming and hints of scarcities and famine. This provides a valuable backdrop to the period leading up to the great Famine which began in 1845.

But there were other periods of crop failure leading to famine and distress on the island. In a report dated 30 June 1835, sent by W. Lewis, chief constable of police, to Major Warburton, inspector general of police, concerning the plunder of a cart load of oatmeal sent by Rev. Hughes, parish priest of Newport to Rev. Connolly, parish priest of Achill, it was stated that

> I hear and from the observations I have made that the greater part of the inhabitants of the island and adjoining districts are in an actual state of starvation and that unless immediate relief be afforded them, the most lamentable consequences may be expected to follow.[62]

There were other instances of famine before the end of the decade and early the following decade. In 1837, there was a great scarcity of provisions and it was hoped that the long, dry and warm spell that summer, with its promise of a good harvest, would alleviate the suffering of the islanders.[63] The next year, 1838, saw a failure of the potato crop and a fund was opened by the Mission for the relief of distress in Achill.

The Mission's accounts for the year ending 31 December 1842 gave details of income and expenditure in respect of a Distress Fund. The income was made up of subscriptions received £301. 18s. 3d., and cash for provisions sold £91. 8s. 11d., making a total of £393. 7s. 2d. The expenditure was

Cash paid to labourers	£199. 16s. 1d.
Cash paid for potatoes, oatmeal and carriage	£147. 17s. 8d.
Cash paid in relieving sick and poor	£ 28. 18s. 9d.
Balance in treasurers hands	£ 18. 14s. 6d.
Total	£ 393. 7s. 2d.[64]

It is likely that the first real harvest from the Mission's farm was in 1837, when it was reported that

> a small field of oats was reaped on our own Mission farm on 22nd inst., the grain is of the finest quality. The ground where it grew was a useless bog three years ago. A limestone quarry, which a friend lately discovered in the immediate neighbourhood of our settlement, will greatly forward our agricultural work, as we find by experience that lime is the best manure for the bogland, indeed it cannot be effectually reclaimed without it. Our potato crop is remarkably productive, and we are happy to say that it is generally so throughout the island.[65]

In his evidence to the Devon Commission in 1844, Nangle stated that when land reclamation was first undertaken by the Mission, 'there was not so much as a cart on the island; there are now several. A plough used in the summer for drilling turnips was introduced last year.' He then gave details of what it cost the Mission to reclaim four acres of bog on Achill. The total cost for this was £81. 16s. 9d. It included the enclosing of the whole area with a turf fence; digging and levelling-in the old bog holes; cutting drains; turf for burning lime and land; cost of lime, including the price of stone carriage, breaking, burning and putting out; second digging and chopping; raising and putting out gravel, burning land, and sticking in seed; manure, and carriage of it to the field (this was the dearest item at £26. 6s. 6d.); digging and chopping furrows, and moulding potatoes; and eight barrels of seed. Nangle's expectation was that through the example set by those who worked on the colony's farms, there would be an improvement in the agricultural practices in the locality.[66]

As the Mission expanded, it had to provide a way for its population to convey its value of civility and 'improvement' to others. Most importantly here was education. In the mid-1830s, very few of even the more respectable farmers could read or write.[67] A society of Baptists, in about 1830, set up a school in Achill which was carried on until the priests stirred up the people against it, and the teacher, with no prospect of success, abandoned his work and left the place.[68] The prospect of schools being opened by the Mission must have been seen as advantageous for the children of the island.

On 23 December 1834, the first school was opened by the Mission in the village of Slievemore and on the very first day forty-three children were in attendance. On the next day, ten more children put in an appearance.[69] Three years later, in his examination before a committee of the House of Lords, Nangle proved that in the spring of 1835 he had established schools in the villages of Dugort, Slievemore, Cashel and Keel which were attended by 420 children.[70] One of the most important reasons for this success was undoubtedly the support of a local teacher and noted Irish scholar, Michael McGreal, a native of Westport and a convert to the Protestant faith.[71] However, three of the schools were quickly broken up because of the 'furious persecution which the priests had raised against them.' It was then expected that there would be an increase in the numbers attending the school in the settlement. This appears to have been the case as the numbers rose from thirty to forty-three in 1835.[72]

By 1839, the numbers had risen and there were 240 children in Mission schools, an increase of thirty-five over the previous year, and the average attendance at Sunday School exceeded 140, not including twenty gratuitous teachers. There were eighty-nine children in the orphan asylum which was opened in the previous year, and of these, ten had been removed since then and two others had died. The orphan asylum was intended to cater for a maximum of one hundred as more than this number was felt to be unmanageable.[73]

There was an increase of ten children in schools in 1842 over the previous year's total of 240. The schools at Dooega and Bullsmouth had been given up, while those at the settlement, on Inishbiggle and Scruffanbuis still continued in operation. It appears that the boy's school at the settlement had not given satisfaction to the local committee, but the children at the other schools had 'made fair proficiency' despite the prevalence of infectious sickness, principally among the young people, which prevailed in the settlement at that time. Nine of the orphan boys were learning different trades in the settlement, and of these, five were able to support themselves without any help from the institution.[74]

In the 1830s, teachers salaries ranged from an average of £20 per annum in the Mission schools to £8 per annum in the national schools, the latter supplemented by gifts of clothing and hospitality from appreciative parents. Pupils attending hedge schools paid fees of between 1s. and 2s. 6d. per quarter for instruction in reading, writing, arithmetic and the Roman Catholic catechism.[75] The national school curriculum also included these subjects with some additions. The Mission schools concentrated on spelling, scriptural reading, writing and arithmetic.[76] The first issue of the *Achill Herald* carried an advertisement for a schoolmaster at one of the Mission schools at a salary of £150 per annum.[77] In addition to better salaries than those enjoyed by national school teachers, five of the Protestant schoolmasters lived rent free in houses built by the Mission.[78]

The National School system was established in 1831 and prior to that time hedge schools provided the only source of education in many of the poorer areas of the country. The establishment of the Mission's schools provided opportunities for those who wished to see their children educated and they attracted the sort of numbers already referred to. Two great opponents of the national system were Dr John MacHale and Edward Nangle, though for different reasons. MacHale was hostile to the system from the beginning and would not allow new schools in his diocese. He opposed their introduction on the grounds that the schools would be non-denominational, school books would have a decidedly British content and the Irish language would not be compulsory.[79] But in the case of Achill, Dr MacHale saw the advantage of the national system. Under his guidance, the local priests set about establishing their own schools in those areas where the Mission schools had already been opened in a vigorous attempt to halt the progress of the latter. Even thirty-five years later, new national schools continued to be opened where Protestant schools were already in operation and vice versa, each vying with the other in a ruthless bid to win over pupils.[80] In the summer of 1835, there were eight full-time schools in Achill – four were Protestant schools supported by the Mission, three were Roman Catholic private subscription schools (later affiliated to the National Board), and one newly established hedge school.[81]

Throughout its growth and expansion, education proved to be one of the most controversial aspects of the Mission. Inevitably, as the Mission expanded, it generated conflict with the Catholic authority in the region. The September 1837 issue of the *Achill Herald* contained an extract from a letter, dated 25 August 1837, written by Rev. Martin Connolly, parish priest of Achill, together with Edward Nangle's vigorous response in which he refuted Connolly's allegations. Connolly claimed that the colony had been in a more prosperous condition two and a half years earlier (presumably in 1835, a year after the arrival of Edward Nangle in Dugort). Nangle dealt with the allegations on three grounds – temporal accommodation, education and attendance on the ordinances of divine worship.

Nangle wrote that the buildings of the colony were unfinished in 1835 and had since been completed. The land which was 'a rugged and unproductive bog had since been converted into fertile gardens.' He said that, as a result of the denunciations by the Roman Catholic clergy against any persons who worked for the colony or sold them provisions, they were obliged to bring in workmen from Westport and also to import provisions at a heavy cost. Now, he claimed there were many more willing to work for them than they could employ and provisions were freely offered for sale at the settlement. He went on 'the produce of our once barren and fruitless mountain will very nearly suffice this year for the support of the population collected around us.'[82]

With regard to education, he drew attention to the Mission's printed reports for 1835, and wrote 'I find that the attendance at our four schools, established in different parts of the island, was reduced from upwards of 400 to about thirty'. He went on to say that 'there are at this time at the settlement, three schools, one for boys, another for females, and a third for infants, and that these are attended by 112 scholars.' Also, there were schools at Dooniver (twenty-one scholars), a fifth was expected to be in operation in the village of Keel and a sixth on Inishbiggle. The total number of children receiving instruction at the time of Rev. Connolly's departure was 133, showing an increase of 100 within the previous two years.

At the time of Rev. Connolly's arrival, their average Sabbath congregation was about thirty. Since that time they had built 'a neat church, capable of accommodating about 150 persons; even this is too limited for our present congregation and we have resolved, in the ensuing spring, to lay the foundation of a church of much larger dimensions.'[83]

Among other matters raised by Rev. Connolly was that natives were being bribed by the Mission to become Protestants and that £12,000 to £14,000 was spent by the Mission on this activity. Again, Nangle referred to printed reports which indicated an expenditure to 31 December 1836 of £4, 378. 0s. 4d. and that by September 1837 only about £5,000 had been spent, and this sum included salaries of ministers, readers, school teachers and land steward, the wages of labourers employed in reclaiming land, school materials, farming stock and implements, rent for school houses, erection of dwellings for ministers and all connected with the settlement. It also included the church and school houses and the expense of an office in Dublin.[84]

In his letter of 25 August 1837, Rev. Connolly stated that 'the number of your apostates from Catholicity in this parish is exceedingly few, considering all the circumstances.' He listed the names of six heads of families together with the number of family members and the corresponding number of children – twelve adults, twenty-three children making a total of thirty-five persons. He also claimed that four individuals and their families had left the colony and returned to his parish. Nangle countered this by saying that sixty-eight and not thirty-five individuals belonged to his congregation and he provided a list of names together with the numbers in each family. It is interesting to note here that the six names on Connolly's list were also contained in Nangle's list. Nangle also stated that his list did not include the number of converts from the Church of Rome and that the number who changed over since the founding of the Mission was eighty-three, and that Connolly's denunciations had been the means of delivering upwards of 151 persons 'from subjection to a man called the pope.' He also claimed that the colony afforded a refuge to nineteen persons who had 'long since abandoned the errors of popery'.[85] Of the whole population residing at the colony, only forty-nine were originally Protestants. It is not clear from Nangle's explanation here exactly how many had converted to Protestantism. It is extremely difficult without accurate records to find the truth in all these claims and counter claims. Suffice to say that there was sufficient movement from the Roman Catholic parish to the colony to alarm both the priests and the Catholic archbishop of Tuam, Dr MacHale.

In May 1839, James Dwyer, who succeeded Connolly as parish priest of Achill, wrote to the editor of the *York Courant*, asserting that all the apostates from his parish at the colony were either excommunicated, adulterers, convicted sheep-stealers, notorious drunkards, etc., and that they were known to Nangle as such.[86] In answer to another claim by Dwyer, apparently denying the existence of the orphan asylum, Nangle listed the names of twenty-one children in the asylum at that time and stating that these were in the charge of William Scuffle. The total number of orphans in the asylum had increased to fifty-six.[87]

Nangle's response to Connolly's letter (which originally appeared in *Freeman's Journal* and in the *Mayo Telegraph*),[88] provides an interesting view of the Mission and its activities in its first few years. In view of the established fact that the vast majority of the population of Achill was Roman Catholic, the question must be asked as to where the forty-nine persons residing at the colony at that time, who were originally Protestant, came from in such a short period of time, at most three years. At that time, there was a coastguard station at Bullsmouth and another at Keel and it is likely the coastguardsmen and their families were all Protestant but they were not all residing at the missionary settlement. As has already been stated, the reliability of the numbers of those who were originally Protestant and those who were converts as claimed by the Mission is open to question.

Impact of the Famine and after

By the year 1845, the missionary settlement at Dugort was at the peak of its development. A thriving village had been established where formerly there was nothing but a barren wasteland and all of this had been accomplished in the space of ten to twelve years. Buildings had been erected, schools and churches opened, land cleared and crops sown and reaped. A hotel had been opened and there were many visitors who came to view the place about which they had heard so much. A dispensary and hospital offered medicines and other support, not only to those in the settlement but to the islanders as a whole. In addition to a shop, there were mills, workshops, a forge, and stables, and transport and communications were improved. Perhaps, one of the settlement's greatest assets was the printing press on which the *Achill Herald* was printed.

In the autumn of 1845, the potato blight arrived in Ireland and moved rapidly across the country, reaching Achill island in November.[1] The measures adopted by the government to deal with the famine which followed the failure of the potato crop in Ireland, were entirely inadequate, due either to excessive bureaucracy or as result of bungling incompetence, or both. The government protection of the interests of those who were opposed to free trade only compounded the effects of the failure of the potato crop, which, at that time, formed the staple diet of the vast majority of people in Ireland, especially those living along the western sea board. The substitute offered was Indian meal or corn. The lack of free trade led to soaring prices for this meal.

As recorded in the *Achill Herald*, a deputation from the village of Cashel on Achill requested that the government should act to put a stop to the exorbitant charges being demanded for meal, and pointing out that one miller was making £100 a day by charging excessive prices. The response from the government was that

> His Excellency said that all merchants in both countries had required that government would not interfere with the course of traffic. The government could not regulate the price between the seller and buyer. It would be an interference with the course of traffic which would not be approved.[2]

The inability of the relief commission, set up by the government, as well as other agencies, to understand the desperate needs of people living in remote parts of the country, and the failure of these agencies in dealing with their problems, led to distress, starvation, and, in very many cases, death. The population of Achill declined by one third in the decade 1841–51. There appears to have been near complete ignorance on the part of officials in Dublin of how people lived in remote districts; ignorance of their way of living; ignorance of how they supported themselves and their families in normal times; ignorance of the lack of amenities, such as roads, which were available in other parts of the country. The government officials, by their instructions to relief committees, made 'landholders and other rate-payers both legally and morally answerable for affording due relief to the destitute poor.' The measures to be adopted by the officers of the government were considered merely as auxiliary to those which it was the duty of the persons possessed of property in each neighbourhood to adopt.[3] They did not take into account the ability or willingness of landlords and other rate-payers to organise and provide such relief.

These measures posed serious problems in the case of Achill Island which was so remote from the centre of government. It should be remembered that, until the bridge across Achill Sound was opened in 1857, there was no land access to the mainland. Sir Richard O'Donnel, landowner of most of the island (the marquis of Sligo owned a small area to the north-east), also had estates around Newport where he had his seat. How was he expected to be responsible for the population of Achill, numbering about 6,000 at the beginning of the Famine period, as well as those living on his estates near Newport?

The *Reports* of the Mission for the years 1845–7 have not survived. The *Achill Herald* and other contemporary or near contemporary writings have to be relied on for information about the response of the Mission to the Famine. As has already been noted, the potato disease was first reported in Achill in November, 1845.[4] By the following February and March (1846), when the pits were opened, it became very clear that the rot was widespread. Many who thought their potatoes quite safe when they placed them in pits, were reluctant to examine them fearing the worst. In most cases, their worst fears were realised and their tubers were a mass of pulp.[5] Fears too were being expressed that the 'seed when sown would also perish and the crop of the ensuing season would be irretrievably lost and the distress and misery of the poor would be awful.'[6] There was already at that time evidence of an increase in the price of provisions, which were 'almost outside the reach of the poor'.[7] In May, potatoes, which might have been had earlier in the year for 2s. had risen to 4s. 6d. and the oatmeal to 17s. per cwt.[8]

Meanwhile, there was a report in the *Achill Herald* that the Mission had been

> enabled to give our people constant employment on the farms belonging to the settlement but as eight pence per day would not suffice to purchase a sufficiency of food, of the very coarsest description, for a family, we have undertaken to feed all the children who have been in

attendance at our schools, during the scarcity. A supply of Indian meal has been sent in here by the government; it is of excellent quality, and makes a very palatable and nutritious diet; it is equal in value, as an article of food, to oatmeal, and is now selling at ten shillings per cwt. This is a great relief; but as the meal is sold, and in no case given gratuitously, the supply is only available to those who have money to purchase it. The demand for labour at this season, in putting in the crops, has given general employment, but the spring work is now finished, and unless employment is given to the poor until the new crop comes in, they cannot maintain themselves.[9]

This was followed by an appeal for funds, stating that 'any funds entrusted to us shall be expended in productive labour on the farms belonging to the Mission; no gratuitous relief shall be given except where the sufferer is unfitted for labour by old age or sickness.'[10] This statement was repeated many times in respect of relief provided by the Mission throughout the period of the Famine and beyond. It should be said here that this was also in line with government thinking and instructions

> gratuitous relief shall be afforded only to those persons who are entirely incapable of giving a day's work, and who have no able-bodied relative on whom they are dependent, and in these cases only in which their reception in the workhouse of the union is, from want of room, impracticable.[11]

In accordance with the recommendation of the relief commission, local relief committees for the temporary relief of the poor of the neighbourhood, were to be set up and were to include clergy of the different religions.[12] In the case of Achill, the first local relief committee was set up in June 1846, with Edward Nangle as chairman, and included Rev. Dwyer, parish priest, and Rev. Monaghan, Roman Catholic curate. The other members of this committee were Rev. E. Lowe, Rev. J. French, Rev. Wm. Burke, Mr J. Campbell, Esq., Don McLoughlin, Esq., J. McLoughlin, Esq., and treasurer – Neason Adams, M.D., and secretary – T.L. Wood. Esq.[13] On 29 October 1846, Dr Adams, the honorary physician to the Mission, wrote to the relief commissioners to say that the local relief committee for Achill had ceased on 15 August, and 'has not been reformed – nor can not I believe'.[14] Dr Adams did not say why the committee collapsed but in the meantime he appears to have endeavoured to provide some form of continuity. The following year, on 13 February 1847, Sir Richard O'Donnel wrote to Dublin to inform the commissioners that a new relief committee had been formed for the electoral division of Achill consisting of John McLoughlin, Dominick McLoughlin, Dr Adams, the Protestant and Roman Catholic clergymen, Robert Savage as secretary and himself as chairman, and that they had appointed Thursday for the days of meeting at the Hotel Achill Sound.[15] Writing in the *Achill Herald* in September 1847, Nangle described the reason for his exclusion from the Achill relief committee. Mr Butler, inspecting officer, called to his house and expressed his desire to a member of Nangle's family that Nangle should join the committee. He was reluctant at first but later agreed and wrote to Butler to this effect but received no reply. However, he attended every meeting of the committee until 13 August when the clerk of the committee informed him that he was not a member.[16] It is possible to speculate that, as the building hired by the government as a depot for the reception and sale of Indian corn was located in the missionary settlement, the priests may have felt they were being by-passed, and may have raised objections to his membership.

The relief committee submitted an application for the making of a road within the island at an estimated cost of £130. This road, it was said, would provide employment and would be of the 'greatest utility to this neigh-bourhood shortening the distance (as well as avoiding many hills) of at least two miles between the post offices of Newport and Dugort.' The hope was expressed that the commissioners would take into consideration that the small amount of subscriptions received (£32 – £20 from Sir Richard O'Donnel, £2 from Nangle and £10 from several Christian friends) was due to the 'scarcity of respectable inhabitants in the locality'.[17]

The relief commissioners' response to this appeal was that a sum of £22 for the building of the road was recommended, and noting that the number of vacancies in the workhouse on 13 June was 900.[18] From the correspondence which ensued, it is clear that the local committee was taken aback by this response and commanded the secretary, T. L. Wood, to write saying that his former letters must have failed to convey an adequate view of the state of want existing in the island or the commissioners would have granted a much larger sum. The sum suggested would not have sufficed to give employment for two days to the 'poor who have neither food nor the means to purchase it.' Wood went on to state that, on 7 July, 275 persons were employed and from that number those who had food or the money to purchase it were carefully excluded from this employment. He also said that until people could gain relief from the growing crop a magistrate and a strong detachment of military should be sent to the island to protect the government stores and other property from 'a population driven from famine to desperation.'[19] In the meantime, Sir Richard O'Donnel gave a sum of £200 for the road. A special grant of £50 was recommended 'for affording employment in Achill,' and the local committee was advised to write to Captain Perceval at Westport for the grant of £22. The Board of Works advanced a loan of £200 for the completion of the road. The loan was to be repaid by the county and the work was put under the supervision of the county surveyor.[20]

By the end of September, the distress was so great that 'instances have occured where persons, on coming to the store for meal, have actually offered to sell their beds, or some other article of furniture, so that the cravings of their starving offspring might for a moment be alleviated.'[21]

Dr Adams, posted the following notice, dated 28 October 1846, around the island

> EACH VILLAGE IN THE ISLAND OF ACHILL WILL LET DR ADAMS KNOW
> BEFORE THE TENTH OF NOVEMBER NEXT, THE EXTENT OF LAND READY,
> OR WILL BE MADE READY FOR SEED RYE, BERE, OR BARLEY, AS
> GOVERNMENT WILL SUPPLY SEED AT COST PRICE. [22]

On 29 October 1846, he wrote to the Relief Commission that

> The hundred orphans will be without food after Monday next; with great difficulty four hundred of meal was procured at Newport and Mr Levingston of Westport writes that he cannot supply the local demand there. I humbly beg that a supply of Indian or Irish meal be sent to the government store on this island that our valuable institution may not be broken up.[23]

Meanwhile, Dr Adams wrote to Dublin enclosing the returns regarding the possibility of land being ready or expected to be ready for rye on the island. He also said that

> three men called on me this morning as sent by sixty-nine others who have been working on a road near this place – complaining that some have been working one week, others a fortnight – and up to this moment have received no wages. These poor creatures all almost unable to walk to their work and when there are stopping under this load.[24]

The following response was received in November

> I am directed to inform you that same having been referred to the Board's officer he reports, 'I beg to state that the labourers in Achill under the most favourable circumstances could hardly have received their first payment before they had worked ten days, the incorrectness of the check list, which had to be returned for revision, consequently were not received by Mr Gillespie the pay clerk till the eighteenth instant, was the cause of an increased delay but I am confident no further time was lost.[25]

This is an example of the sort of delay endured by people who had worked to provide for themselves and their families and were at that time actually starving.

On 19 November, 1846, the *Lydney Lass*, a large schooner freighted with a valuable cargo of provisions, sailed from the port of Dublin. The cargo was destined for storage at the settlement, 'but the benefit of purchasing food at a fair price will not be limited to persons connected with the missionary establishment but will be extended to the whole district.' The Relief Association paid for the freight of the vessel and the cargo was purchased by Nangle, partly with funds subscribed and partly with money raised by his own security. The cargo was insured.[26]

A few months earlier, Nangle made an appeal for funds 'to freight a large vessel with Indian meal at Liverpool : at that time, the meal which now costs £15 per ton might have been had for £10, and the cargo might have been landed with little risk upon the beach, which cannot be done now that winter has set in.' As the government intimated its intention to keep a supply of meal in Achill, and having taken a store at the Mission for that purpose, Nangle did not proceed with this plan. However, it appears no adequate supply of meal was kept on the island; and the store was frequently without any sort of food.[27] Over the next number of months, Nangle expressed his frustration at the lack of assistance and support from government agencies in the pages of the *Achill Herald*.

As the year wore on, there were complaints that the rot had attacked the growing crop which boded ill for the harvest later in the season. What little there was that could be harvested would only have provided partial relief for about two months. In many areas across the island, there was a total failure of the crop.[28] In the November 1846 issue of the *Achill Herald*, Dr Adams wrote about the naked labourers on the island of Achill. He said that numbers of poor creatures attended the dispensary unable to continue on public works for want of clothing. For six or seven months they had not been able to purchase a single article, and were now disposing of their pigs, poultry, sheep and lambs, and even blankets had been sold to procure food. Yet, he went on, 'carts with provisions pass through the island, not only unmolested, but have been assisted by the islanders. A frieze frock coat, costing seven or eight shillings, would enable a poor man to support himself and family for the winter.'[29]

In December 1846, Dr Adams made another appeal for frieze and brogues, noting that he had already distributed thirty-two frock coats and waist-coats, seven monkey-jackets, and thirty-six pairs of brogues.[30] These figures increased in January to 139 frock-coats and waist-coats, nineteen monkey-jackets, and 165 pairs of brogues having been distributed.[31] He closed his subscription list for this charity the following April.[32]

Undoubtedly, the strain of coping with the outcome of the famine must have taken its toll on individuals in the Mission, especially in the case of Nangle. In December 1846, Edward Nangle addressed the friends and supporters of the Achill Mission

My dear friends, – the great increase of correspondence and other business occasioned by the famine, together with the shattered state of my health, rendering it utterly impossible to reply to each of your kind communications separately, I take this means of assuring you of my grateful sense of the kindness which prompts you to send me such liberal assistance towards alleviating the sufferings of our poor fellow countrymen in the district about which I am more immediately interested.[33]

There was a belief among many evangelicals, like Nangle, that the Famine was visited on the country because of the sinful nature and practices of the Roman Catholics. Writing in the *Achill Herald* he made the following address to Roman Catholics under the heading 'The Famine'

To the Roman Catholics of Ireland in general, and of Achill in particular – Fellow countrymen, – Surely God is angry with this land. The potatoes would not have rotted unless He sent the rot to them; God never can be taken unawares; nothing can happen but as he orders it.[34]

The Famine increased in intensity during this time. The distress in some of the villages was so great that the poor were endeavouring to maintain themselves on the limpets they gathered from the rocks and boiled seaweed.[35] According to a report in the *Achill Herald*, January 1847, the Mission gave employment in the previous month, of December 1846, to 4,458 labourers, of which 2,006 were Roman Catholics. They also gave two meals daily to upwards of 600 children, including 100 orphans.[36] In view of the fact that the population of Achill was believed to have been about 6,000, the number being given employment in the middle of winter seems very great. However, in the February issue of the *Achill Herald*, the figures of those employed in January were 2,192 labourers, of whom 740 were Roman Catholics and 1,452 were Protestants. By way of explanation, it was noted that this was an aggregate number giving an average number of 100 men employed per day. It appears that the total number was divided by the number of days in the month, excluding Sundays, giving the average number who received daily employment. Because of a heavy fall of snow in February, there were four days when people could not work.[37] The figure given for the number of Protestants employed seems high, but may be accounted for by an increase in the number of those who recanted and who may have been nominally classified as Protestants. Between 27 October, 1844 and 3 May 1846, there were 186 such recantations recorded.[38] There may have been many more but were not recorded in the register.

There appears to have been a problem in the month of February when the feeding of 600 children was partially suspended for some time as all the Mission's supply of Indian corn had been used up, but on being allowed to purchase at the government store, the Mission was able to resume this work.[39] In March, it was claimed that there were 950 employed on government works, 214 on Mission farms and 1,266 children being fed two meals a day consisting of Indian corn stirabout.[40] There is no way of verifying the accuracy of all the numbers quoted above. It has to be remembered that the *Achill Herald* was used as one of the principal methods of attracting funds for the Mission and the figures may have been stated with this end in view.

The month of March saw an improvement in the supply of Indian meal which was on sale at the government store. Two landings of supplies arrived at the Missionary settlement – one the *Expedition of Milford*, carrying sixty tons of food, and five tons of seed oats, and the *John of Dublin* with thirty-six tons of food, three tons of guano and a ton of seed potatoes, the former being escorted by government steamer from Blacksod Bay with the police also in attendance to prevent the plunder of the cargo.[41] The plundering of cargoes was a constant hazard while the Famine lasted. Markets and freights as well as the cost of insurance had greatly increased, the same money buying less than had been possible a few months earlier.[42]

Despite the government supplies and those of the settlement, there was still very great distress among the people as is illustrated by the following entry in the *Achill Herald*

> The sufferers need not tell their tale of woe, their pale faces, emaciated forms, and dejected countenances are eloquent of misery. We have yet had no deaths, of which hunger could be said to be the *immediate* cause, but the mortality rate in the island is greatly above the ordinary average; more internments have taken place in our burial ground within the last two months than during the last two years before that period, and we are warranted to state on the authority of the honorary physician of our dispensary, Dr Adams, that the disease which carries off so many originates in the insufficiency and unwholesome quality of the food. No one viewing the matter at a distance can realise the difficulty of feeding 6,000 persons in a remote district, of difficult access, on imported food, which that people cannot purchase except they receive wages from employment provided for them.[43]

Dr Adams described how heart-rending it was to see the roads covered with bloated figures, or emaciated frames tottering on to procure a scanty supply of food or going to the dispensary for medicine, advice and nourishment. At that time of the year, the roads should have been full of cheerful boys and girls mounted on their ponies, going for sea-weed for their potato beds. Dr Adams noted that cases of fever, dropsy and dysentery were becoming more frequent and that hitherto he had noted the numbers but that now it was impossible to maintain such records.[44]

In the months of April and May 1847, it appears that little or no sowing was done on the island, other than at the settlement, probably for lack of seed or money to purchase seed. An application to the commissariat general for a steamer to convey 100 tons of seed potatoes to be sold to the natives was turned down even though the Mission was to supply the seed. This project was abandoned. Failure to sow seed that year meant that the islanders would be without food in the following year. It was pointed out that the land was not suitable for the growing of grain and that the islanders did not 'understand the cultivation of green crops'.[45] Daily employment was provided by the Mission to 154 persons that month. 1,323 children were fed daily in their schools and had this not been done many would have died of starvation.[46]

On 28 May, Nangle wrote an angry letter to T.N. Redington, Under Secretary for Ireland, complaining about the neglect by those who were entrusted with the distribution of out-door relief in the district

> The depot at the village of Cashel is eleven miles distant from some of the people who have to apply for relief and after travelling so great a distance it is quite uncertain that their wants will be supplied. *For the last six days* there has been no food in the depot. The suffering of those who depended on it for the supply of their daily food is consequently doubtful. I found sixty families yesterday in the village of Dunevir in a state of actual starvation and to leave them for that humble death I was obliged to give half a stone of Indian corn from our own store to each house.[47]

Outdoor relief under the new poor law was being distributed but had not as yet reached the whole population, and there were many areas which could never be reached. There was still no sowing of the land. The Mission tried to persuade people to make a large sowing of turnips and even offered to let them have the seed at half price or even gratuitously.[48] The dilemma was that those who were needed for sowing had to work on the public works in order to earn money to buy food to survive. Nangle described this as 'fatal misman-agement.'[49] By contrast with the rest of the island, the Mission made a large sowing and it was expected that they would have more food than their own people could consume.[50] A sloop arrived on the sixth of May with twenty tons of seed potatoes but, although they were offered for sale at cost price, there were no takers and they had to be sowed on the Mission farms.[51]

About this time, Edward Nangle became incensed about a comment written by a Mr G.E. Burke, believed to be an officer in the employment of the Board of Works, in the visitor's book of the hotel at the settlement. Mr Burke commented

> . . . that although English charity supplies the poor of this island with the means to live, I am astonished that *English generosity* could require

the ignorant people to abandon the principles in which they were
brought up and the creed which they understand for 'food'. Were the
English people placed as the Irish are, how would they like that any
other nation should call on them to give up the faith of which they are
justly proud, in order that they should be provided with food, the
Moslem for the Christian.[52]

Not unusually for him, this brought an indignant response and denial from
Edward Nangle in the pages of the *Achill Herald*.

While Nangle was considering this affront to his Mission, Dr Adams was
reporting on the health of the people around him. He said that the sick, aged
and infirm were not the only ones seeking support. The cry for food was
almost universal. Those who were previously considered able were now
seeking relief in the form of tickets which were required for employment on
public works. The mournful cry from morning to night, without ceasing,
around their windows and doors, was – 'give me a ticket – give me a ticket,'
'myself and family are starving,' 'dying of hunger.' Few people were now
employed on public works. Many of their neighbours who were formerly
'endeavouring to starve *the devils* out of the island,' were now employed on the
colony's farms.[53] According to Dr Adams fever and dysentery were knocking
at almost every door leaving whole families prostrate, but the former, while
general, was not assumed to be of a very malignant type.[54] The following
month he was reporting that fever, dysentery and anasarcous swellings were
very general – the former not having increased in severity.[55]

During the month of June 1847, the extension of outdoor relief had alleviated
the suffering of many of the poor families, but there was a shortage of food in
places where this relief had not yet reached. Children at the Mission schools only
received one meal per day instead of two meals as heretofore.[56]

While the crops on the Mission farms, where some twenty-one tons of
French, Dutch and Spanish potatoes had been planted, were not only healthy
but luxuriant,[57] the same could not be said of the island generally. Little or
nothing had been done by way of agriculture up to that time, for a number
of reasons, including very wet weather which would have prevented the
burning of the land in preparation for sowing. Attempts were being made to
sow some turnips.

Burke's criticism of Nangle's methods of dispensing relief was not the only
such criticism. Mrs Asenath Nicholson, an American widow, felt she had a
'divine calling to work among the Irish,' and her mission was to bring the
Bible to the Irish poor. She journeyed through Ireland in 1844 and 1845 for
the purpose of personally investigating the conditions of the poor. Her
recollections are recorded in *The Bible in Ireland or Ireland's welcome to the
stranger*, and the *Annals of the Famine* which deals with her relief programme
in 1847. Having heard a great deal about Mr Nangle and the Achill Mission,

she was anxious to see for herself the place which had been described to her as 'a little oasis, where the wilderness has been converted into a fruitful field.'[58] But Mrs Nicholson's welcome at the settlement was not what she expected. Apparently her reputation had preceded her. It was nearly sunset when she arrived and as there were no lodgings in the colony, she was directed to a 'respectable tidy house kept by Molly Vesey.' She described how she walked and waded through deep sand. 'At the hilltop were huddled together kraals of rough stone, flung together without mortar, without gables, and circular at the top.' At Molly Vesey's she found a cow in the kitchen, a man smoking in a corner, a pot boiling, a bed unfit for human occupancy, made up of a bench, a table, a chair, and a barrel. There was a bedstead in the room, but this was for the man smoking in the corner. When she enquired if Molly intended to put a man into the room that night, the latter replied in the affirmative. Her indignation was aroused and not entirely against Molly. In the colony, she had been told that Molly Vesey was not only a respectable woman, but that she kept a respectable house. It appears that it was a shebeen. She moved out the following morning.[59]

During her time in the colony, she visited the three schools there.[60] Later she sent her letters of introduction to Nangle. The next day, after noon, the weekly lecture at the colony was held in the schoolroom. She was left standing for some time before being offered a bench to sit on. Nangle ignored her completely.[61] Later she did get to see him. He handed her back her letters without saying a word. She asked a number of questions about the colony. In a few words, he told her of its prosperity and that it has exceeded all expectations. At some point Mrs Nangle came into the room and appears to have behaved in quite a rude manner to Mrs Nicholson.[62] Writing about the Mission afterwards, Mrs Nicholson acknowledged that much had been done and that the neat white cottages and pleasant road made a striking contrast with the huddles around Molly Vesey's house. But she said that

> I have looked in the cabins of many of the converts in Dingle and Achill, and though their feet were washed cleaner, their stools scoured whiter, and their hearths swept better than in many of the mountain cabins, yet their eight pence a day will never put shoes on their feet, convert their stools into chairs, or give them any better broom than the mountain heath for sweeping their cabins. It will never give them the palatable well-spread board around which their masters sit, and which they have earned for them by their scantily-paid toil.[63]

Mrs Nicholson, writing about her second visit to the settlement in December 1847, spoke of the 'fallacy of distributing a little over a great surface.' In the eleven schools maintained by the Mission, she said the 'scanty allowance given to the children once a day, and much of it bad food, kept them in lingering want, and many died at last.' She went on to state that

Mr Nangle had many men working in his bogs, near Mr Savage [the hotel proprietor at Achill Sound], and so scantily were they paid – sometimes but three pence and three pence-halfpenny a day – that some at least would have died but for the charity of Mrs Savage. These men had families to feed and must work till Saturday, then go nine miles into the colony to procure the Indian meal for the five day's work. This he truly called giving his men employ.[64]

Mrs Nicholson also wrote that another 'sad evil prevalent in nearly all the relief shops was the damaged Indian meal.' She said 'such meal a good American farmer would not give to his swine for physic, and when the half-starved poor, who had been kept all their life on potatoes, took this sour, mouldy harsh food, dysentery must be the result.'[65] Nangle refused to meet her or effect any reconciliation with her.[66] Mrs Nicholson's criticism of Nangle and, especially of Mrs Nangle's treatment of her, were responded to by Nangle when he castigated her in an article in the *Achill Herald* about six weeks after her first visit.[67]

Writing in the *Report* of the Mission, Nangle noted that the Famine continued into 1848 and that a large portion of the land remained uncultivated. He stated that he had had talks with a Dublin merchant who had recommended the importation of Indian grain direct from America. The merchant suggested that, even though Nangle said he had no money, he could reimburse him when the friends of the Mission supplied funds for the purchase of the cargo. Rather naively, Nangle agreed to the purchase and signed the order on those terms. However, when the cargo arrived, the merchant would not release it until payment was received and held Nangle personally responsible. Nangle and Rev. Charles Seymour, rector of Achill parish, then spent three months calling on friends in Ireland and England, preaching and seeking to raise funds to meet this debt. Nangle was of the opinion that the cargo of corn was the means of saving many lives and that it had supplied about 1,800 children daily with food since the previous December (1847), and had supported a daily average of seventy labourers on Mission farms.[68]

There had been a number of incidences of famine since the arrival of the missionaries, but they could not have anticipated the catastrophe that struck the island in 1845. In the midst of its prosperity, the Mission could not have failed to notice the tragedy unfolding outside its very doors. Indeed it was seen as an opportunity to advance its cause and increase the number of converts to Protestantism. It is interesting to observe here, that at the height of the Famine in the year 1847, the Hibernian Bible Society provided 278 Bibles, 1,400 testaments and 1,475 portions. These, and a further 3,000 portions from the Trinitarian Bible Society, were distributed, principally through the Mission's schools.[69] The feeding of large numbers of children in

Mission schools provided Nangle with an ideal opportunity of teaching them the Bible in addition to the other subjects. He claimed that this was not being done without the consent of either the children or their parents. The fact that he was providing food for the children, albeit a limited amount, could be classified as moral blackmail as the alternative for both children and parents was almost certain starvation. He made no secret of his intention to have all the children in the orphanage and the asylum for destitute children brought up as Protestants. An indication of the desperate position in which many people found themselves is shown in the record of the numbers who recanted between 1844 and 1846. The charge of 'souperism' against Nangle persists to the present day. The fact that the government store was located in the settlement certainly gave him an advantage over the Roman Catholic clergy who perforce had to turn a blind eye to his activities during the Famine period. They had no alternative since so many people were starving on the island. Nevertheless, it has to be said that the efforts made by Nangle to raise funds to enable him to purchase Indian meal and seed for distribution certainly saved many lives that would otherwise have been lost.

In September 1849, 400 children were confirmed by Bishop Plunket. According to Nangle, only twenty-eight of this number were children of Protestant parents. The remaining 372 were converts, the majority children in Mission schools, but also some older persons.[70] This may well point to successful proselytising on the part of the Mission during the Famine period.

It was stated by Nangle, at the end of 1848, that there were thirty-four schools in operation, under the supervision of Charles Seymour. Edward Lowe, who was attached to the settlement, was in charge of the orphan institution. Seymour's curate was Rev. T. Loughnan. Divine Service was celebrated and the Gospel preached at the settlement, in Mweelin, where a new church was built, Bullsmouth and Achill Sound. A fifth station was opened in Dooagh (about five miles from the settlement). Besides the Sunday services, there were week-day lectures in six other villages where Sunday services were not held. Not many of the peasants attended these services. At the time, Nangle complained that, not only had they to contend with the 'bigotry and hypocrisy of Roman Catholics,' but also the 'coldness and indifference and enmity of nominal Protestants; and the circulation of falsehoods designed to disparage our missionary work.'[71]

The accounts for the year ended 31 December 1848 make interesting reading. Among the items on the income side are receipts from the colony farms, including rents, receipts from the Mweelin and Inishbiggle farms, receipts from the mail car, printing office, forge and hotel; sales in the shop, sales of views of Achill and sales of building materials. It also included the sale of government stock and cattle. On the expenditure side, a wreck and hooker were purchased. There were expenses incurred in respect of the colony, Mweelin and Inishbiggle farms as well as one and half year's rent for the Dublin office. The overall expenditure for the year amounted to £2,688. 14s. 11d. Because of Nangle's increasing infirmities, the temporal affairs of the Mission, subject to the committee, were placed in the hands of the agent, Thomas Langley.[72]

The parish was now served by three ministers – Charles Seymour the rector of the parish lived in Mweelin, Edward Lowe had charge of the congregation and schools in settlement, and Patrick McCloskey residing at Achill Sound had charge of the southern and eastern portions of the parish. There was yet another example of proceeding with a building without sufficient funds being in place. Charles Seymour was personally responsible for the cost of building a church at Achill Sound and appeals for funds were issued in an effort to meet the costs.[73]

Writing in May 1850 Nangle reported that the feeding of 1,800 children, along with the salaries paid to their teachers and the rent of school houses cost £2,134 for the year, or little more than £1 for each child, and that a considerable portion of this sum was derived from the Mission's farms. The total amount contributed for temporal relief was only £1,394 and of this sum £315. 18s. 10d. was spent on relief given in labour or gratuitously. In fact, most of this sum was used for clearing and fencing about eighteen or twenty acres which were producing crops for the Mission.[74]

It is clear that, with the whole of the island of Achill suffering from the effects of the Famine, many people turned to the Mission either for their own survival or that of their children. Something of the impact of the Famine can be seen in the changes in the population of the settlement. As has already been noted, Dugort was divided into Dugort, Dugort East and Dugort West in the census returns from 1841 onwards but separate figures were not given for the settlement. Comparing the figures for 1851 with those of 1841 as set out in the second chapter, table 1, there was an increase of 132 (fifty-eight males and seventy-four females) in Dugort by 1851. However, in Dugort East, there was a decrease of nine (seven males and two females). There was a greater decrease in Dugort West where the total was 110 (sixty-seven males, forty-three females).[75] It is likely that the population as a whole increased between the years 1841 and the onset of the Famine in 1845, therefore the figures may not reflect the true impact of the Famine.

Table 6. Housing in Dugort, 1841–51

	1841			1851		
	Inhabited	Uninhabited	Total	Inhabited	Uninhabited	Total
Dugort	31	11	42	47	8	55
Dugort East	6	1	7	6	–	6
Dugort West	67	3	70	49	–	49
Totals	104	15	119	102	8	110

Source: Census of Ireland.[76]

There was an increase of sixteen in the number of inhabited houses in Dugort in the decade 1841–51, while the number of uninhabited houses decreased by three (table 6). There was a decrease of eighteen in the number of inhabited houses in Dugort West during the same period. This decrease may have been related to the Famine and to migration into Dugort itself.[77]

From 1838–61, a total of 331 baptisms were solemnised in Dugort. Of these, 182 were from the Colony/Dugort area, 130 from outside the Colony/Dugort area, and nineteen others whose records were unclear.[78] For the sake of convenience, the numbers have been broken down into four periods as shown in table 7.

Table 7. Baptisms in Colony, 1838–61

Year	Colony/Dugort		Outside Colony		Unclear
	M	F	M	F	
1838–43	34	22	15	19	9
1844–49	33	31	22	16	4
1850–55	19	22	15	9	5
1856–61	15	6	17	17	1
Totals	101	81	69	61	19

Source: Achill parish baptismal register.[79]

Table 8. Baptisms and burials in Colony, 1838–61

Colony Year	Baptisms		Burials (includes orphans)	
	M	F	M	F
1838–43	34	22	14	7
1844–49	33	31	25	6
1850–55	19	22	7	11
1856–61	15	6	3	4
Totals	101	81	49	28

Source: Achill parish baptism and burial register.[80]

By comparing the figures in tables 7 and 8, it becomes clear that in the Colony/Dugort area, the number of baptisms exceeded the number of burials by almost 50 per cent in the case of both males (fifty-two) and females (fifty-three). As this study is concerned with persons identified with the Colony/Dugort area, those who came from outside this area were not considered. It is worth noting that in three of the four periods set out, male baptisms exceeded those of females. The same applies to burials in the case of the first two periods. There was a high number of male burials between the years 1845–49

– 1845 (4), 1846 (1), 1847 (11), 1848 (5), and 1849 (2). The highest numbers recorded were for 1847 and 1848 which coincided with the Famine. Of the seventeen males who died between 1845 and 1849, there were four deaths in each of the age groups – years 1–10, 31–40, 41–50, and 51–60. There was one death in the age group 11–20 plus two from the orphan colony, and none in the 21–30 age group. Table 9 shows a breakdown of the age groups for male and female burials during the period 1838–61.

Table 9. Age profile of burials

	Colony/Dugort		Orphans	
	M	F	M	F
Under one year	–	1	–	–
Years 1–10	10	5	5	–
Years 11–20	6	7	2	1
Years 21–30	1	1	–	–
Years 31–40	6	1	–	–
Years 41–50	7	3	–	–
Years 51–60	5	1	–	–
Years 61–70	2	–	–	–
Years 71–80	–	–	–	–
Years 81–90	1	–	–	–
Sub-totals	38	19	7	1
Age not given	4	8	–	2
Totals	42	27	7	3

Source: Achill parish register of burials.[81]

By combining the numbers for the colony and the orphans, there were forty-nine males and thirty female burials. It is worth noting that twenty-one children had died by the age of ten years and a further sixteen by the age of twenty years. No women lived beyond the age of sixty, in fact fifty-five years was the oldest recorded for a woman. Two men reached the age of sixty, one sixty-five, one seventy and one ninety years. The reason for this disparity between the ages of men and women may have something to do with the primitive living conditions, poor diet and large families in the case of women. For instance, Mrs Nangle, who died at the age of fifty, had a total of ten children, five of whom died either at birth or shortly thereafter. There is no clear reason why some men lived beyond sixty years. Even Nangle, who suffered from ill health for most of his life, was eighty-three when he died.

There are two registers for marriages solemnised in the church in Dugort, one is held in the Representative Church Body Library and the other in the

Church of Ireland in Westport. There is a little overlap between the two, one having less information than the other. In studying these registers, much the same periods as used for the baptisms and burials have been set out. The number of marriage records considered was 102 and most of the entries were quite readable. The highest number of marriages took place between 1844 and 1855 after which there was a considerable drop in numbers. As the marriages took place in Dugort, the figures have not been confined to those in the colony only.

Table 10. Condition of persons marrying between 1845 and 1861

Year	Widower	Widow	Bachelor	Spinster	Not given
1845	1	–	3	4	4
1846	3	1	4	6	–
1847	1	–	1	2	–
1848	1	1	2	2	–
1849	1	2	8	7	–
1850	5	6	10	9	2
1851	–	–	7	7	–
1852	–	2	7	2	3
1853	–	1	2	1	–
1854	1	1	3	3	–
1855	–	–	1	1	–
1956	–	–	–	–	–
1857	–	–	4	4	–
1858	–	–	1	1	–
1859	–	–	2	2	–
1860	–	–	1	1	–
1861	–	–	1	1	–
Totals	13	14	57	53	9

Source: Achill parish marriage register.[82]

From table 10, it can be seen that the highest numbers of persons getting married in the aftermath of the Famine, was eighteen in 1849 and thirty-two in 1850, after which the numbers dropped to fourteen in each of the years 1851 and 1852 and to four in 1853. It may well be that, because of the Famine, persons intending to get married delayed doing so, and emigration may have been a factor in the later years. There was a slight rise to eight in 1854, but the numbers dwindled in the following years. The number for 1846 was fourteen and this dropped to four in 1847.[83]

Taking the period 1845–50, the only years for which details of age and condition on marriage were recorded, there were twelve widowers, ten widows, twenty-five bachelors, twenty-six spinsters and one girl of sixteen years, giving a total of seventy-four persons. There was only a small number of younger persons (17–20 years) marrying in the years 1848–50; in 1845 there were seven spinsters and one bachelor, and in 1846, one bachelor and two spinsters marrying in this age group. Most of those who married in the years following the Famine were either in the 21–25 or 26–30 age groups (table 11). This may be an indication of a desire to rebuild the community after the Famine years.

Table 11. Marriage by age group in Dugort

Year	21–25 age group	26–30 age group	Total
1845	2	2	4
1846	4	4	8
1848	2	5	7
1849	5	7	12
1850	6	3	9

In the year 1847, only one marriage was recorded between a widower (aged forty) and a spinster (aged twenty-eight).
Source: Achill parish marriage register.[84]

Table 12. Principal occupations of fathers, 1845–50

Year	Labourers	Others	Total
1845	2	2	4
1846	7	–	7
1847	1	–	1
1848	4	2	6
1849	3	6	9
1850	9	6	15
Total	26	16	42

Source: Achill parish marriage register.[85]

As will be seen from table 12, and referring to table 5 for the period 1838–45, the principal occupation remains that of labourer, perhaps indicating that activities associated with agriculture still predominated.

The decline in the number of marriages in the decade following the Famine, as outlined in table 10, had serious consequences for the population of the settlement. This and other factors led to a re-evaluation of the future of the whole enterprise.

6. The Colony Achill, *c.*1890. (Source: NLI, Wallace Collection, ref, LROY 168).

In the aftermath of the Famine, the Mission faced a series of new challenges to adapt its work to a changing environment. For some time, as has already been noted in the second chapter, the committee of the Achill Mission was concerned about the future of its holdings because of the inability of the landlord, Sir Richard O'Donnel, to grant a lease for more than three lives or thirty-one years, and some fifteen years of that lease had already been used up. The committee members were concerned that, at the expiration of the lease and because of the successful development of their property, a higher rent would be demanded which might deter the directors of the Mission from taking a renewal of the lease. They were also concerned that all their costly improvements might, in time, be alienated from the Mission and might even fall into the hands of Roman Catholics and that the Mission would have been totally destroyed.[86] When, therefore, Sir Richard O'Donnel's property came into the Encumbered Estates Court, which was set up in 1848–9 to facilitate the sale of bankrupt estates, an appeal for funds was made to the friends and supporters of the Mission to enable them to purchase the lands in the immediate vicinity of their settlement. Initially, Nangle stated that he had concluded a contract for the purchase of about 9,000 acres, at sixteen years purchase, according to the Valuation. £5,000 was required for this and he had procured a loan for that sum at five per cent interest, with the privilege of repaying the principal by instalments of £1,000. He stated that they had at that time about £400 in government stock to the credit of the trustees.[87]

Their supporters responded so generously to the appeal that it was decided to purchase, not just a part of the estate, but the whole island, with the exception of three townlands on the eastern coast, and the island of Inishbiggle and two townlands on the mainland containing 2,000 acres. However, the funds raised were not sufficient to cover the agreed cost of £17,500 for the entire purchase. The amount raised was only £10,500. Three English gentlemen came to the rescue. In return for £7,000, they were to receive a share of two-fifths and the Mission was to retain three-fifths of the estate.[88] The three were William Pike, Samuel Holme and Thomas Brassy. Pike subsequently bought out the other two and then became one of the major landlords of the island.[89]

The purchase by the Mission was completed in April 1851 and was vested in the following trustees

> The Hon. Somerset Maxwell, the Right Hon. Joseph Napier, M.P., George Alexander Hamilton, Esq., M.P., and the Rev. Edward Nangle.[90]

Unfortunately for the Mission, because of legal arrangements it would not benefit from the purchase of the estate for a number of months. In time, it was found that the income derived from the rents of the estate did not render the Mission independent of any further assistance for its support.[91] Writing many years later, Nangle noted that difficulties arose when those who supported the purchase of the estate 'considered themselves absolved from the obligation of contributing any further pecuniary aid to the Mission.'[92] The delay in deriving any return from the capital invested added to the problems facing the Mission. According to Nangle, 'it was also evident that, in consequence of the utter impoverishment of the tenantry by the protracted famine, it would be years before the estate could yield enough to support the Mission.'[93] The Mission was threatened with ruin.

About this time, the Society of Church Missions to the Roman Catholics of Ireland, which then had ample funds at its disposal, at the request of Edward Nangle, took charge of the whole missionary work in Achill, including the clergymen, scripture readers, school teachers and the entire support of the Mweelin training school.[94] The Irish Church Missions, as it was now called, paid all the expenses connected with the ministry and the education work of the schools.[95] It also erected, at considerable expense (£300), extensive buildings at Mweelin for the training school, and appointed W. J. Stewart as master there.[96] By 1855, the Irish Church Missions was dissatisfied with the suitability of the Mweelin training school building. It was decided, with the approval of the bishop of Tuam (Plunket) who was present at the meeting, that a careful selection of the pupils most likely to become useful agents or schoolmasters would be made and to transfer them to the Society's training school in Dublin as soon as possible and to close the Mweelin school. It was also decided to make the building at Mweelin available for other of the Society's missionary work in Achill.[97] However, this was found to be impossible and the female orphans of Achill were allowed to occupy it for the time being to prevent its dilapidation.[98] As the Irish Church Missions was now in charge of the missionary work, a temporal relief committee was formed with Dr Adams as president and treasurer to look after the temporal affairs of the settlement.[99]

In July 1856, the Achill committee was notified by the Irish Church Missions of the Society's intention to withdraw from Achill on 31 December of that year. Efforts were made through negotiation to induce them to change their mind, but these were unsuccessful and the final decision was communicated to the Achill Mission in November. There had been a serious falling away of the funds of the Irish Church Missions making it impossible for them to continue their work in Achill.[100] The Irish Church Missions had a number of reasons, in additional to financial ones, for giving up the Achill Mission. These included the expenditure of £7,396, the purchase by the Achill Mission of the most of Achill Island and an apparent conflict of interest between the Achill Mission's answering to the Dublin committee (which still existed) and to the Irish Church Missions. Also, direct appeals were made to parties in England by the Achill Mission for the support of its various activities thereby giving the impression of separateness between the Achill Mission and the Irish Church Missions.[101] At a general meeting in October, it was resolved to make over to the Achill Mission that management which the Irish Church Missions had received in 1852, with effect from 31 December 1856.[102]

When the Irish Church Missions withdrew from Achill, the schools and scripture readers were left without any support other than that derived from funds for which Edward Nangle made appeals. Consequently, the number of schools was reduced from fourteen to seven and the scripture readers from twelve to four. The agricultural school was closed for want of funds and arrangements were made to provide the apprentice boys with situations elsewhere. There were twenty orphan girls, who were children of Roman Catholic parents or converts, in the orphan institution.[103] Once there had been 100 boys in this institution, but it appears there were none at this time.

As had been done many times in the past, the Achill committee made an appeal for funds to support its activities but without the same success it had in the past. It is worth comparing the total income and expenditure for the year 1857 with the totals for the year ending 1850. In 1850 the total income and expenditure amounted to £3,144.10s. 0d. compared with a total for the year ending 1857 of £1,270. 5s. 4d.[104] This financial decline mirrored the general falling off of support for the Mission.

In addition to the financial difficulties experienced by the Mission in the 1850s, a number of other developments had a profound effect on its future. In

June 1850, Mrs Nangle died in Dublin. She had been ill for six years and had spent the last two in Dublin. Her remains were brought back to Achill where she was buried. It appears that in the early part of her life she had had an opportunity to acquire skills in account-keeping, and because of this experience she was able to save the Mission from the expense of employing a book keeper.[105] Her life in Achill and the loss of five of her children must have taken its toll on her health.

The year 1851 saw the purchase of the Achill Mission estate completed. In either 1850 or 1851, Edward Nangle was appointed rector of Achill in succession to Charles Seymour who had become provost of Tuam. In 1852, after eighteen years working in Achill, Nangle was appointed rector of Skreen, County Sligo, in the diocese of Killala. In the same year, he remarried and his second wife was Sarah, daughter of the Rev. Cuthbert Fetherstonhaugh, rector of Hacketstown, County Carlow.[106] In June of that year, Nangle's third child, Matilda (Tilly), died unexpectedly on a visit to Dublin. Like her mother, her remains were brought back to Achill for burial.[107] Nangle continued at Skreen until 1879, but it is said that he returned every summer for about three months and he retained a house in the settlement. He continued his contributions to and editing of the *Achill Herald*. From time to time he endeavoured to provoke controversy but without the same success he previously enjoyed. He retired from all active work in 1873 and died in Dublin on 9 September, 1883 aged eighty-three years.[108] He was buried in Dean's Grange cemetery.[109]

On 18 December 1855, Mrs Isabella Adams, wife of Dr Neason Adams, also died. It was exactly twenty years earlier on the very same date that she arrived on Achill for the first time.[110] Dr and Mrs Adams had no children. In the statement of expenditure for the year 1857, there is record of an 'award' to Dr Adams of £200 for his house in Dugort. From this, it may be assumed that he left Achill in same year. He died in 1859 and both he and his wife were buried in Knockbride, County Cavan.[111]

Most commentators speak of the humanity of Dr Adams and refer to him as the 'St Luke of Achill.' He left a thriving practice in Dublin, at the request of Nangle, to minister in the Achill Mission in circumstances which must have been far removed from his previous way of life. While he was deeply committed to the philosophy and aims of the Mission, he nevertheless extended help and care to the entire population of the island, irrespective of their religious beliefs. In all of this he was supported by his wife to whom he appears to have been very devoted. He never received any remuneration for his services and had built his house at his own expense. It is likely that, by acting as a counter balance to the rigidity of Nangle's approach, he contributed to the 'success' of the Mission and to its survival for so long. There is no doubt that his tireless work during the Famine years helped save many lives. Dr Adams's death in 1859 saw the real end of the missionary activity.[112]

The Protestant population of Achill was subjected to a continual drain from emigration, but it was believed to have been considerably above 600 in 1858. In the 1860s the population of the Mission stagnated and then fell off. The population figures for the three townlands of Dugort, taken from the censuses of 1841 to 1901, shows a decline in all three. There was an increase of thirteen in 1851 and the total decrease from that census to 1901 was 430 persons. The greatest decrease was in the decade 1851–61 when the population fell by 270. In the following decades, the decrease was more gradual with falls in population of fifty-three by 1871, eleven by 1881, fifty by 1891 and forty-six by 1901. In Dugort itself the population fell by 361 between 1851 and 1901. Between 1891 and 1901, the population of Dugort fell by thirty-nine which was attributed to removals and the discontinuance of the coastguard station.[113] According to a report submitted to the Dugort Vestry Meeting held on 17 April, 1871, the number of enrolled church members was 255.[114] The total population of the three townlands in the census for that year was 395. In the 1880s, the tide of emigration reduced the ranks of the Mission. Between April and May 1883, forty-two members of the Church of Ireland parish left Achill for Canada, America and Australia.[115] By 1901, there was only a total of ninety-two persons listed under the heading Protestant/Episcopalian for the three townlands – Dugort thirty-five males and thirty-seven females, Dugort East two males, and Dugort West nine males and nine females making a total of forty-six males and forty-six females.[116]

A number of other factors led to the final collapse of the Mission. In the 1860s, two of the trustees, Sir Joseph Napier and George A. Hamilton were in dispute with Nangle over the disbursement of the estate's income which they felt should be used to improve the lot of the peasantry. A lawsuit ensued over this and, when Nangle and his chief supporter, Bishop Plunket of Tuam, were successful, both men resigned.[117] Many of the Mission's supporters were disappointed over these resignations, especially that of Napier who was held in high regard.[118] But this was followed by other difficulties. The first of these was land agitation, followed by the Land Act of 1881, which reduced rents by between 30 and 40 percent, the Arrears Act which cancelled much of what was due in arrears and then the 'No rent manifesto' of the Land League.[119] An appeal for help was made to the Irish Society, which had been responsible for the training and supplying of Irish teachers and scripture readers over the years, but even the Society could not raise the minimum expenditure of £600 needed per annum.[120] After this, the missionary work went into almost total abeyance. The small number of Protestants in the three townlands of Dugort, as enumerated in the 1901 census, is perhaps a reflection of failure of the Mission to convert the population of the island of Achill to Protestantism and of its own ultimate demise.

Nangle was virtually forgotten, even in his lifetime, and today, the missionary settlement or colony at Dugort is viewed merely as a curiosity.

Conclusion

The history of the Achill missionary settlement is a complex one, and within the limitations set for this study, it was only possible to delineate some part of it. It was the creation of the Rev. Edward Nangle, a single-minded evangelical missionary, who was vehemently opposed to all matters relating to the Roman Catholic religion. He saw his mission in life as a calling to rescue Roman Catholics from the idolatry, superstition and the errors of Rome, and of converting them to the Protestant faith. In this he may be said to have singularly failed. One of the methods by which he sought to achieve this objective was the provision of education, especially for the young of the island as he believed they would be more amenable to change than their parents. The fact that, when he opened his first school on 23 December, 1834, forty-three children attended followed by ten more the next day, points to a desire on the part of the local people to have their children educated. It also indicates the neglect of such provision at the time which Nangle exploited by quickly establishing other schools around the island. But his motive was primarily to educate the children and to convert them to the Protestant faith and, inter alia, their parents also. He was vehemently opposed in this by the Roman Catholic clergy who counteracted his efforts, firstly, by establishing schools where he had already opened them, and, secondly, by introducing a system of exclusive dealing which deterred parents from sending their children to the Mission's schools. The opening of an orphan asylum or refuge at the settlement was perhaps the most controversial innovation and the one which was of most concern to the Roman Catholic clergy. Nangle made no secret of his intention to have children in the orphanage brought up as Protestants. This blatant proselytising angered the clergy. However, the Catholic clergy turned a blind eye, when children in their hundreds were sent to Mission schools during the Famine, despite the fact that they were being taught the Bible and Nangle's known intentions.

From the beginning, Nangle had the support of some powerful evangelical clerics, such as the Rev. Robert Daly, who became bishop of Cashel in 1843, and Dr Power le Poer Trench, archbishop of Tuam, in whose diocese Achill lay, and who gave him considerable moral support. He was also supported by other well-known evangelicals, including Rev. W. B. Stoney, who was rector of Newport when he first went ot Achill and later rector of Castlebar.

The acquisition of a site at the foot of the Slievemore mountain near the old village of Dugort from Sir Richard O'Donnel, owner of most of Achill

Island, and its development as a missionary settlement from barren land to a thriving village in a period of ten to twelve years, was quite remarkable. But it was not achieved without controversy, and very strong opposition came from the Roman Catholic archbishop of Tuam, Dr John MacHale and the priests he sent to the island. The system of 'exclusive dealing' had serious consequences for the Mission in both financial and material terms. It meant that supplies had to be imported from Westport and elsewhere on the mainland at considerable expense. Workers too had to be brought in to assist with the work at the settlement and this may have increased the number of converts. Nothwithstanding these measures, the settlement developed quite quickly from small beginnings and secondary settlements on Inishbiggle and at Mweelin were also established.

By mid-1840s, when the missionary settlement had been firmly established, with its village and schools, reclaimed farmland and luxuriant crops, it had a promising future ahead of it. Then the great Famine struck the island in the autumn of 1845. The Mission's response to this tragedy was towfold. It was seen as an opportunity to advance its cause and increase the number of converts to Protestantism. This was borne out by its determination to provide food for the children attending its schools and the numbers who recanted their religion. The efforts of Nangle and his fellow missionaries to endeavour to alleviate the worst features of the Famine by importing grain and providing work for the peasants has to be commended, even if the motives were not straightforward. The Mission also responded to this crisis in a number of other ways. It succeeded in having the government relief store located in one of its buildings which it hired out for that purpose. As well as feeding large numbers of children attending its schools, also in its orphan asylum, it provided work on its farms and through government works; it imported Indian meal and seed, and provided some relief for those too old or unfit for work. However, if the type of work provided is considered carefully, it will be noticed that all of the improvements were ultimately for the enhancement of the Mission and its satellites.

The Mission also made repeated appeals for funds to its supporters and distributed aid whenever possible. Yet the method of such distribution came in for much criticism from such persons as Mrs Asenath Nicholson and G.E. Burke, the latter levelling a serious accusation of proselytising in return for aid. There is no doubt that, in the case of the children in the orphan asylum, and later in the asylum for destitute children, the intentions were clear. According to Bowen, the charge of 'souperism' against Nangle remains to this day. The view put forward by Nangle and his missionaries was that the potato disease was a visitation from God, angered by the sinfulness of the Roman Catholics.

The fact that Nangle did not ultimately succeed in his objective of converting the population to Protestantism was due to a number of reasons. He probably did not understand the mentality of the people of the island and their attachment to their Catholic faith, despite the neglect of their clergy over the years. When the worst of the Famine was over, many of those who recanted their religion during that period, returned to their original beliefs. The 1901 census of population, showing how few Protestants remained in the Dugort townlands, is likewise evidence of the failure of the missionary effort. Famine and emigration also played a part in this decline.

Another feature of Nangle's activity on the island was the introduction of new farming practices. The collapse of native farming during the Famine period, when the potato blight struck and the lack of an alternative, was in sharp contrast to the success achieved by the Mission's farms. The natives had no alternative crop to the potato and when faced with starvation, sold almost everything they possessed to feed themselves and their children. They even sold their fishing nets and so were unable to avail of the rich fishing around their island. They flocked to the settlement in the hope of getting some relief. The success of the farms belonging to the settlement and attempts to get the people to change their methods of farming are to the credit of the Mission.

Intermingled with the physical development of the settlement was the story of the two people most associated with it, Nangle and his friend Dr Neason Adams, honorary physician to the Mission. Nangle established the Achill Mission, and, for most of his long life, was directly or indirectly associated with it. While he was the initiator, founder, director, spiritual as well as temporal, of the missionary settlement he was assisted for over twenty years by his friend, Dr Adams. The religious and secular activities of the Mission went hand in hand.

The gift of a printing press from supporters in London and York, was one of the greatest assets of the Mission. Experienced printers were employed and apprentices were enabled to learn the craft. From the first, Nangle, as editor and main contributor for most of the years the *Achill Herald* was published, used it to publicise his ideas, answer his critics, promote or deal with controversy, and above all, to generate funds for his Mission. It had a wide circulation throughout the United Kingdom and as far away as Canada and India. Through its pages, Nangle portrayed a settlement that was withstanding the forces of evil and as such deserving of support. The main objective of his outpourings every month was to ensure a constant inflow of funds for the Mission, which, for nearly eighteen years, was very substantial. However, in spite of it strenuous efforts, the Mission had to rely on outside help for its maintenance. Even though the Mission received assistance from Dublin for the salaries of its missionaries, teachers and scripture readers, it was almost completely dependant on voluntary contributions for its survival. Such was the pace of development that very often the construction of buildings was proceeded with before financial arrangements were in place. This led to frequent appeals, either through the *Achill Herald* or by means of fund-raising visits to England and other parts of Ireland.

Perhaps the most elaborate scheme of this nature was the purchase in 1851 of most of Sir Richard O'Donnel's estate on Achill island through the Encumbered Estate Court. Initially, it was only intended to purchase about

9,000 acres, but when the funds for this exceeded expectations, it was decided to purchase the entire lot as well as two townlands on the mainland. The idea was to frustrate any Roman Catholic plans to purchase lands which the Mission had leased and on which the settlements were built. Had such plans been fulfilled, it would have led to the destruction of the Mission altogether. The agreed price for the expanded area amounted to £17,500 but the Mission only succeeded in raising £10,500. Three English gentlemen, William Pike, Samuel Holme and Thomas Brassy made up the difference of £7,000 in return for three small estates. The Mission then ended up with three-fifths of Sir Richard O'Donnel's estate on Achill and with the two townlands on the mainland, and the trustees of the Achill Mission estate thus became the major landlord of Achill island. However, because of the impoverished state of the tenants on the estate following the Famine, there was little prospect of a return on the investment in terms of rents for many years to come. This combined with the decline in support from those who had contributed to the purchase price, and who now felt that they had absolved themselves from providing further funds for the maintenance of the Mission and its estate, placed the Mission in serious financial difficulties and threatened its very survival.

In 1852, the Mission was rescued by the Irish Church Missions society which took over responsibility for the schools and missionary work and the training school in Mweelin, leaving the temporal activities to the trustees of the Achill Mission estate. However, in 1856, when the Irish Church Missions were unable to continue supporting the work in Achill, they closed down the training school in Mweelin and transferred its activities to Dublin, and at the same time withdrew from any involvement in the Achill Mission. Control of the Achill Mission was then returned to its trustees.

Nangle was appointed rector of Skreen, County Sligo, in 1852. He had spent eighteen years in Dugort, establishing, promoting and developing his missionary settlement, and had defied the expectations of those who believed he would be run out of the island within six weeks of his arrival. The fact that the settlement survived for so long was due in part to Dr Adams but also to Nangle's management skills. With a management structure in place, it meant that, despite his long absences, either for the purposes of raising funds or because of ill health, the settlement continued to function. His ability to attract support, which was translated into a very considerable inflow of funds in response to his various appeals, was evident from the fact that he was able to clear the debt incurred in respect of the importation of a cargo of grain within a short period. By all accounts, he had a strong personality which he used to good effect when confronting his Roman Catholic opponents. But the loss of his management skills and personality when he departed for Skreen may have accelerated the decline of the Mission.

Dr Adams had come with his wife to live in conditions far removed from what he was used to in order to minister to the needs of a people who lacked any form of medical support. He clearly had private means because he was able to build a house at his own expense and never received a salary during his years in Achill. He established the first dispensary and hospital on the island. Up to that time, the nearest dispensary was in Newport, twenty-five miles away. During the Famine, he appears to have assumed responsibility when the local relief committee collapsed in August 1846. In spite of the fact that he fully supported the philosophy of the Mission, he never differentiated between those who lived in the settlement or were associated with it and the people of the island as a whole. Many would attribute the fact that the Mission lasted as long as it did to Dr Adams. He left the island within a couple of years of his wife's death in 1855, and he himself died in 1859. According to Bowen, the real missionary life of the Achill Mission ended with his departure. While the charge of 'souperism' still remains in the case of Nangle, no such charge was ever made against Dr Adams.

Appendix 1

The following is the set of rules drawn up for the management of the Achill and Inishbiggle mission as agreed by the Board of Guardians in Dublin and the Court of Local Management at Achill, 1 January, 1840.

1st   That the directors shall in future take the position of guardians – with the Rev. E. C. Pendleton their secretary.

2nd   The guardians are to continue their co-operation as usual and to afford their advice and assistance in all matters referred to them by the court of local management, the secretary to summon a board for that purpose.

3rd   The guardians to have power to add to their numbers, and on the death, or resignation of one guardian, the secretary to summon a board for the purpose of electing a successor, not fewer than three members present.

4th   That all remuneration to all members of the court of local management be left to the decision of the guardians, and all other matters in which the members of the court shall be personally concerned.

5th   When a guardian shall honour the Mission with a visit, the court shall be summoned, at which sitting and adjournment of the same, the guardian to preside, to afford him every possible opportunity of investigating the secular and religious establishments connected with the United Mission.

6th   The court of local management to consist of the first missionary who shall be chairman, the second missionary, the physician, the steward, Captain Dyer, R.N., and a secretary, with power to add to their numbers.

7th   The court to hold regular weekly meetings to investigate and determine, as far as in their power, all matters connected with the Mission, to keep a regular account of income and expenditure, open at all times to the inspection of the guardians and friends of the Mission, to preserve all vouchers for money paid and chairman to sign all drafts on treasurer.

8th   The second missionary and physician to act as treasurers.

9th   They are to receive all money arising from donations, subscriptions, collections, etc., from sale of produce of farms, and therefrom to pay all legal demands on the Colony, having received a written order from the chairman of court of local management.

10th   That all subscriptions or donations for the Mission shall be paid to Messrs. La Touche, Castle Street, or to Rev. E.C. Pendleton, 16 Upper Sackville Street, Dublin. The receivers shall on the 1st day of each month transmit to one of the treasurers by letter of credit on Westport bank the amount of money received with a list of names and residences of contributors.

11th   That a report of the Mission with a correct list of subscribers, and a statement of income and expenditure be made in the month of February annually.

12th   That two gentlemen unconnected with the board of guardians or court of local management be appointed annually to audit the accounts before publication.

(Signed) E.C. Pendleton – Secretary guardians
William M. Bourke – Secretary court of local management

Appendix 2

Year	Amounts contributed				Totals		
	£.	s.	d.		£.	s.	d.
1835	739.	11.	8	(Ireland)			
	923.	0.	1	(England)	1,662.	11.	9
1836	234.	8.	7	to Nangle	234.	8.	7
1839	128.	7.	11	(Ireland)			
	910.	9.	5	(England)			
	283.	18.	10	Mission's local fund			
	341.	11.	7	Orphans			
	25.	14.	1	Dispensary			
	69.	10.	2	House of Recovery			
	436.	19.	7	Distress	2,196.	11.	7
1842	1,552.	17.	0	Achill Mission a/c			
	388.	19.	10	Orphans			
	301.	18.	3	Distress			
	42.	17.	2	Dispensary	2,289.	12.	3
1843	1,499.	11.	10	Achill Mission a/c			
	544.	0.	9	Orphans			
	45.	0.	0	Dispensary	2,088.	12.	7
1844	1,083.	2.	4	Achill Mission a/c			
	253.	1.	6	Orphans			
	53.	5.	3	Dispensary	1,389.	9.	1
1848	1,478.	14.	5	A.M. a/c incl.temporal relief			
	2,087.	19.	5	Nangle's collection England			
	168.	16.	5	Orphans			
	9.	5.	0	Priests's asylum	3,744.	15.	3
1849	1,311.	3.	11	Achill Mission a/c			
	1,294.	4.	7	Temporal relief			
	12.	10.	10	Priests's asylum			
	3.	0.	0	Fishing pier			
	55.	19.	8	Dispensary	2,776.	18.	3
1850	2,429.	8.	4	A.M. a/c inc. temporal relief			
	40.	7.	3	in Achill	2,469.	15.	7
1857	398.	14.	5	Achill Mission account			

All the above amounts were taken from the accounts which accompanied the *Reports* of the Mission with the exception of the last which was included in the statement issued by the Achill committee in January 1858. (Note – amounts were taken to the nearesrt penny).

Appendix 3

1   Dr Adams: house, porch at rear, stables, store house, piggery and privy. Infant school house, church and school house.

2   Rev. E. Nangle: house, addition at rear, porch to same, pantry; lean-to houses study, part used as storeroom for books; cow sheds at rear, piggery, stables.

3   Rev. E. Lowe: house, addition at rear, porch to same, scullery, pantry.
    The guardians of the Achill Mission settlement: warehouse or shop (30 ft x 18).

4   William Pope: hotel, cart house and stables, shed at rear of same, barn (34ft).
    The guardians of the Achill Mission : printing office (40 ft).

5   Patrick Hughes: house (27 ft).

6   School house (76.6 ft). storehouse at rear(19 ft); sundries not roofed.

7   Orphan house (123 ft); orphan house (46 ft).

1   Fever hospital: porch at rear, temporary sheds at rear, piggery and porch at rear

2   Rev. E. Nangle: Corn and tuck mill (45 ft), kiln at end.
    Margaret Reynolds, house, stores, cow house, turf house.
    James Rankin: house, scullery, turf house.

Source: NAI, House books for Dugort.

Notes

ABBREVIATIONS

AM   Achill Mission
CSORP   Chief Secretary's Office Registered papers
ICM   Irish Church Missions
IHS   *Irish Historical Studies*
JGAHS   *Journal of the Galway Archaeological and Historical Society*
NAI   National Archives of Ireland
OS   Ordnance Survey
RCBL   Representative Church Body Library
RLCF   Relief commission files

Notes:
The outrage papers are referred to according to the year of the relevant report.
In the case of parliamentary papers, the pagination cited is that of the printed pagination of each parliamentary paper.
The dates of the *Annual Reports* of the Achill Mission (referred to as *Reports*) are those of the published dates, but most refer to the preceeding year's affairs.
The spelling of place-names has been modernised except where they are used in quotations to give a sense of the contemporary style.

INTRODUCTION

1   Theresa McDonald, *Achill Island, archaeology – history – folklore* (Tullamore, 1997), p. 18.
2   Information courtesy of the Director of the National Library, Dublin.
3   *Report from the select committee appointed to inquire into the Irish miscellaneous estimates relative to public works.* H.C. 1829, iv, p. 127.
4   *First report of the commissioners of public instruction, Ireland, with appendix to first report,* H.C.1835, xxxiii, pp 32d–33d.
5   Rev. Joseph D'Arcy Sirr, D. D., *A memoir of the honourable and most Rev. Power Le Poer Trench, last archbishop of Tuam* (Dublin, 1845), p. 597.
6   Desmond Bowen, *The Protestant crusade in Ireland, 1800–70: a study of Protestant-Catholic relations between the Act of Union and Disestablishment* (Dublin, 1978), p. xii.
7   Bowen, *The Protestant crusade*, p. xiii.

8   H.P.R.Finberg, *The local historian and his theme* (Leicester, 1965), p. 9.
9   Rev. James Greer, *The windings of the Moy with Skreen and Tireragh* (Dublin, 1924), pp 99–112.
10 *General valuation of rateable property in Ireland, Counties of Mayo and Sligo, valuation of the several tenements in the Union of Ballina* (Dublin, 1856), (hereafter referred to as Griffith's valuation).

BEGINNINGS

1   Henry Seddall, *Edward Nangle: the apostle of Achill; a memoir and a history* (London, 1884), p. 27.
2   Most sources give the year of Nangle's birth as 1799. However, an entry in Edward Nangle's Bible, in his own handwriting, gives the date of his birth as 25 November 1800. F. E. Nangle, in collaboration with J.F.T Nangle, *A*

short account of the Nangle family,
(privately printed, 1986), p. 25; p. 46, n.
33.

3 Patrick Comerford, 'Edward Nangle
(1799–1883): The Achill missionary in a
new light', in *Search, a Church of Ireland
Journal*, xxii no. 2 (Winter, 1999),
p. 124.

4 Seddall, *Nangle*, p. 32.

5 Irene Whelan, 'Nangle and the Achill
Mission, 1834–52' in R. Gillespie & G.
Moran (eds.), '*A various country*', *essays
in Mayo history 1500–1900* (Westport,
1987), pp 118–9; Seddall, *Nangle*, p. 36.

6 Seddall, *Nangle*, p. 40.

7 Seddall, *Nangle*, pp 38–9.

8 Seddall, *Nangle*, p. 41.

9 Seddall, *Nangle*, p. 44.

10 Comerford, 'Nangle', p. 125.

11 Seddall, *Nangle*, p. 39.

12 Nangle, *A short account*, p. 25, n. 33.

13 Seddall, *Nangle*, p. 46.

14 Whelan, 'Nangle', p. 120.

15 Comerford, 'Nangle', p. 125.

16 Seddall, *Nangle*, p. 47.

17 Seddall, *Nangle*, p. 50.

18 Seddall, *Nangle*, p. 50.

19 Seddall, *Nangle*, p. 51.

20 Seddall, *Nangle*, p. 51.

21 Seddall, *Nangle*, pp 52–3.

22 Kenneth McNally, *Achill*, (Newton
Abbot, 1973), p. 123.

23 Seddall, *Nangle*, p. 53.

24 Seddall, *Nangle*, p. 54.

25 Seddall, *Nangle*, p. 55.

26 Seddall, *Nangle*, p. 55.

27 Desmond Bowen, *The Protestant crusade
in Ireland, 1800–70: a study in Protestant-
Catholic relations between the Act of Union
and Disestablishment* (Dublin, 1978), p. 74.

28 Bowen, *The Protestant crusade*, p. 76.

29 Bowen, *The Protestant crusade*, p. 74.

30 *Achill Herald*, October 1864.

31 Seddall, *Nangle*, p. 56.

32 Seddall, *Nangle*, p. 56.

33 Seddall, *Nangle*, p. 56.

34 Seddall, *Nangle*, p. 57.

35 *Achill Herald*, October 1864.

36 Bowen, *The Protestant crusade*, p. 53.

37 Seddall, *Nangle*, p. 59.

38 *Achill Herald*, October 1864.

39 *Achill Herald*, July 1837.

40 Seddall, *Nangle*, p. 59.

41 Seddall, *Nangle*, p. 60

42 *Achill Herald*, July 1837.

43 Seddall, *Nangle*, p. 60.

44 Nangle, *A short account*, p. 26.

45 *Ballina Impartial*, 7 January 1833.

46 Nangle, *A short account*, p. 27.

47 Irish Church Missions leaflet
*Commemorating the 150th anniversary of
the founding of the Achill Mission,
1834–1984*.

48 Seddall, *Nangle*, p. 61.

49 Seddall, *Nangle*, p. 88.

50 Seddall, *Nangle*, p. 61.

51 Seddall, *Nangle*, p. 62.

52 *Achill Herald*, October 1864.

53 *2nd Report of the missionary society for Achill
and other islands off the Irish coast* (July,
1836), p. 1. (hereafter cited as *2nd Report*)

54 *2nd Report*, p. 6.

55 *6th Annual Report of the Achill Mission for
the year ended 31 December, 1839 with a
report on the orphan refuge for the same
period* (printed at the Mission press by
William Pugh, 1840), p. 6, (hereafter
cited as the *6th Report*).

56 *6th Report*, p. 6.

57 *9th Annual Report of the Achill Mission for
the year ended 31 December, 1842 with a
report of the Achill orphan refuge up to the
same period* (*Achill Mission* press, 1843),
p.45, (hereafter cited as the *9th Report*).

58 *10th Annual Report of the Achill Mission for
the year ended 31 December, 1843 with a
report of the Achill orphan refuge up to the
same period* (Achill Mission press, 1844),
p. 27, (hereafter cited as the *10th Report*).

59 *Achill Herald*, January 1844.

60 *11th Annual Report of the Achill Mission for
the year ended 31 December, 1844, with a
report of the Achill orphan refuge up to the
same period* (*Achill Mission press*, 1845),
(hereafter cited as the *11th Report*).

61 Mr. and Mrs. S. C. Hall, *Ireland: its
scenery and character* (3 vols, London,
1843), iii, p. 395–6.

62 Hall, *Ireland*, p. 396.

63 *2nd Report*, p. 55.

64 *2nd Report*, pp 41–43.

65 *A list of all the subscriptions received for the
Achill Purchase Fund, 1851*; *17th Report*.

66 Seddall, *Nangle*, p. 158.

67 Seddall, *Nangle*, pp 307–8.

68 Seddall, *Nangle*, p. 309.

69 *Dr. MacHale in Achill. The old religion
defended. A sermon preached, on the
occasion of Dr. MacHale's visit to Achill, in*

the *Mission church*, by Rev. E. Nangle, A.
    B. (Dublin, 1838), p. 17.
70 *Achill Herald,* June 1839.
71 *6th Report*, p. 4.
72 *Achill Herald,* July 1837.
73 Seddall, *Nangle,* p. 73.
74 Seddall, *Nangle*, p. 63.
75 NAI, Outrage papers, Mayo, 1835.
76 Seddall, *Nangle*, p. 89; NAI, Outrage
    papers, Mayo, July 1837.
77 NAI, Outrage papers, Mayo, August
    1837.
78 Seddall, *Nangle*, p. 90.
79 NAI, Outrage papers, Mayo, February
    1837.
80 NAI, Outrage papers, Mayo, 1837.
81 NAI, Outrage papers, Mayo, 1839.
82 NAI, Outrage papers, Mayo, September
    1838.
83 Seddall, *Nangle*, pp 116–7.
84 Whelan, 'Nangle', 124; Seddall, *Nangle*,
    p. 116.
85 *Achill Herald*, March 1839.

EVOLUTION OF THE SETTLEMENT
1833–1845

1 *Achill Herald,* January, 1856.
2 *2nd Report*, p. 6.
3 *2nd Report*, p. 22.
4 *2nd Report*, p. 55.
5 *2nd Report*, p. 36.
6 *2nd Report*, p. 6.
7 *2nd Report*, p. 7.
8 *2nd Report*, p. 8.
9 *2nd Report*, p. 7.
10 *6th Report*, p. 3.
11 *Achill Herald*, August, 1838.
12 *Achill Herald,* August, 1838.
13 *6th Report*, p. 5.
14 Seddall, *Nangle*, p. 117.
15 *6th Report*, p. 5.
16 *6th Report*, pp 5–6.
17 *6th Report*, p. 7.
18 *6th Report*, pp 29–30.
19 *6th Report*, pp 5–6.
20 Kenneth McNally, *Achill* (Newton
    Abbot, 1973), p. 98.
21 *6th Report*, p. 11.
22 *6th Report*, p. 11.
23 *6th Report*, p. 32.
24 *6th Report*, p. 32.
25 *6th Report*, pp 38–40.

26 *9th Report*, p. 3.
27 *9th Report*, p. 3.
28 *9th Report*, p. 30.
29 *9th Report*, p. 42.
30 *Achill Herald*, April, 1865.
31 McNally, *Achill*, p. 95.
32 Register of marriages, Dugort, Achill,
    1838–89 (book I), in Holy Trinity
    Church of Ireland, Westport, County
    Mayo (hereafter cited as Register of
    marriages).
33 Register of baptisms, Dugort, Achill,
    1838–66 (book I), in Holy Trinity
    Church of Ireland, Westport, County
    Mayo (hereafter cited as Register of
    baptisms).
34 Register of baptisms.
35 Valuation Office, Cancelled Books,
    1855 and 1859.
36 *9th Report*, pp 3–4.
37 *9th Report*, p. 5.
38 *Achill Herald*, May 1841.
39 Seddall, *Nangle*, pp 345–6.
40 *9th Report*, p. 10.
41 *10th Report*, p. 5.
42 *11th Report*, p. 1.
43 *11th Report*, p. 1.
44 *9th Report*, p. 30.
45 *9th Report*, p. 4.
46 *Achill Herald*, January, 1844.
47 *First Report of the commissioners of public
    instruction in Ireland*, H.C. 1835, xxxiii,
    p. 32d.
48 *Achill Herald*, October, 1864.
49 *Report by the Lord's select committee
    appointed to inquire into the progress and
    operation of the new plan for education in
    Ireland; together with minutes of evidence*,
    H.C.1837,viii, part 1, pp 425–33.
50 Seddall, *Nangle*, p. 62.
51 *9th Report*, p. 45.
52 *10th Report*, p. 28.
53 *The census of Ireland for the year 1851, Part
    I: showing the area, population and the
    number of houses, by townlands and
    electoral divisions, Vol. IV, Province of
    Connaught, County of Mayo*, H.C.
    1852–3, xcii, p. 568, (hereafter cited as
    Census of Ireland, 1851).
54 Griffith's *Valuation of Tenements for
    Counties Mayo and Sligo*, 1856.
55 *Census of Ireland, 1851*.
56 Register of baptisms.
57 Register of baptisms.

58 Register of burials, Dugort, Achill, 1838 onwards, in Holy Trinity Church of Ireland, Westport, County Mayo (hereafter cited as Register of burials).
59 Register of marriages.
60 Register of marriages.
61 Register of baptisms.
62 NAI, Outrage papers, Mayo, 1835.
63 *Achill Herald*, July 1837.
64 *9th Report*, p. 39.
65 *Achill Herald*, August, 1837.
66 *Report from Her Majesty's Commissioners of inquiry into the state of the law and practice in respect of the occupation of Ireland*, H.C. 1845, xix, 1 (hereafter cited as the Devon Commission), pp 430–33.
67 McDonald, *Achill Island*, p. 110.
68 Desmond Bowen, *Souperism: myth or reality, a study in souperism* (Cork, 1970), p. 89.
69 Seddall, *Nangle*, p. 66.
70 Seddall, *Nangle*, p. 66.
71 Seddall, *Nangle*, pp 67–8.
72 *2nd Report*, p. 8.
73 *6th Report*, p. 8.
74 *6th Report*, p. 2.
75 McNally, *Achill*, p. 186.
76 McNally, *Achill*, p. 188.
77 *Achill Herald*, July 1837.
78 McNally, *Achill*, p. 188.
79 McDonald, *Achill*, p. 116.
80 McNally, *Achill*, p. 187.
81 McNally, *Achill*, p. 186.
82 *Achill Herald*, September 1837.
83 *Achill Herald*, September, 1837.
84 *Achill Herald*, September 1837.
85 *Achill Herald*, December 1836.
86 *Achill Herald*, May 1839.
87 *Achill Herald*, May 1839.
88 *Achill Herald*, September 1837.

IMPACT OF THE FAMINE AND AFTER

1 *Achill Herald*, November 1845.
2 *Achill Herald*, October 1846.
3 NAI, RLFC 3/1/5452, November 1845.
4 *Achill Herald*, November 1845.
5 *Achill Herald*, February 1846.
6 *Achill Herald*, March 1846.
7 *Achill Herald*, March 1846.
8 *Achill Herald*, May 1846.
9 *Achill Herald*, May 1846.

10 *Achill Herald*, May 1846.
11 NAI, RLFC, 3/1/5452, p. 3.
12 NAI, RLFC, 3/1/5452, p. 1.
13 NAI, RLFC, 3/1/3627.
14 NAI, RLFC, 3/2/21/33, Ref. 6887.
15 NAI, RLFC, 3/2/21/33, Ref. 11137.
16 *Achill Herald*, September 1847.
17 NAI, RLFC, 3/1/3627, 24 June 1846.
18 NAI, RLFC, 3/1/3862.
19 NAI, RLFC, 3/1/4098, 7 July 1846.
20 NAI, RLFC, 3/1/4292, 15 July 1846.
21 *Achill Herald*, September 1846.
22 NAI, RLFC, 3/2/21/33.
23 NAI, RLFC, 3/2/21/33.
24 NAI, RLFC, 3/2/21/33, 16 November 1846.
25 NAI, RLFC, Mayo, 7852, 30 November 1846.
26 *Achill Herald*, November 1846.
27 *Achill Herald*, November 1846.
28 *Achill Herald*, October 1846.
29 *Achill Herald*, November 1846.
30 *Achill Herald*, December 1846.
31 *Achill Herald*, January 1847.
32 *Achill Herald*, February 1847.
33 *Achill Herald*, December 1846.
34 *Achill Herald*, February 1847.
35 *Achill Herald*, February, 1847.
36 *Achill Herald*, January 1847.
37 *Achill Herald*, February 1847.
38 Register of baptisms, marriages and burials, Dugort, Achill, (book I), in Holy Trinity Church of Ireland, Westport, County Mayo (cited hereafter as register of baptisms, marriages and burials).
39 *Achill Herald*, February 1847.
40 *Achill Herald*, March 1847.
41 *Achill Herald*, March 1847.
42 *Achill Herald*, February 1847.
43 *Achill Herald*, March 1847.
44 *Achill Herald*, March 1847.
45 *Achill Herald*, April 1847.
46 *Achill Herald*, April 1847.
47 NAI, CSORP, Distress 5915.
48 *Achill Herald*, May 1847.
49 *Achill Herald*, May 1847.
50 *Achill Herald*, May 1847.
51 *Achill Herald*, May 1847.
52 *Achill Herald*, May 1847.
53 *Achill Herald*, May 1847.
54 *Achill Herald*, May 1847.
55 *Achill Herald*, May 1847.
56 *Achill Herald*, June 1847.

57 *Achill Herald*, June 1847.
58 Asenath Nicholson, *The Bible in Ireland: Ireland's welcome to the stranger* (London, 1926), p.254.
59 Nicholson, *The Bible in Ireland*, p. 256.
60 Nicholson, *The Bible in Ireland*, pp 256–7.
61 Nicholson, *The Bible in Ireland*, p. 259.
62 Nicholson, *The Bible in Ireland*, pp 260–1.
63 Nicholson, *The Bible in Ireland*, pp 262–3.
64 Asenath Nicholson, *Annals of the Famine in Ireland*, ed. Maureen Murphy (Dublin, 1998), p.105.
65 Nicholson, *Annals* p. 105.
66 Asenath Nicholson, *Lights and Shades of Ireland*, part iii (London, 1850), p. 313.
67 *Achill Herald*, July 1845.
68 *15th Report*, p. 4.
69 *15th Report*, p. 7.
70 *15th Report*, p. 5.
71 *15th Report*, p. 3.
72 *15th Report*, p. 3.
73 *15th Report*, p. 6.
74 *16th Report*, p. 1.
75 *Census of Ireland* for the years 1841 and 1851.
76 *Census of Ireland* for the years 1841 and 1851.
77 *Census of Ireland* for the years 1841 and 1851.
78 Register of baptisms, marriages and burials.
79 Register of baptisms, marriages and burials.
80 Register of baptisms, marriages and burials.
81 Register of baptisms. marriages and burials.
82 Register of baptisms, marriages and burials.
83 Register of baptisms, marriages and burials.
84 Register of baptisms, marriages and burials.
85 Register of baptisms, marriages and burials.
86 *Report of Achill committee*, 1858, p.1.
87 *16th Report*, p. 2.
88 Seddall, *Nangle*, p. 190; *17th Report*, p. 3.

89 McNally, *Achill*, p. 27
90 Seddall, *Nangle*, p. 190; *Report of Achill committee*, 1858, p. 1.
91 *Report of Achill committee*, 1858, p. 1.
92 *Achill Herald*, November 1886.
93 *Achill Herald*, November 1886.
94 Irish Church Missions records, 23 April 1852, ref. 860, and 27 April 1852, ref. 879.
95 Seddall, *Nangle*, p. 190.
96 ICM, records, 9 and 25 June 1852, ref. nos. 928–9.
97 ICM, records, 8 June 1855, ref. 1988.
98 ICM records, 28 September 1855, ref. 2067.
99 Seddall, *Nangle*, p. 190.
100 *Report of Achill committee*, 1858.
101 ICM, records, 22 August 1856, ref. 2390.
102 ICM, records, 1 October 1856, ref. 2403.
103 ICM, records, 1 October 1856, ref. 2403.
104 ICM, records, 1 October 1856, ref. 2403.
105 *Achill Herald*, July 1850.
106 Nangle, *A short account*, p. 26
107 Seddall, *Nangle*, pp 193–4.
108 Seddall, *Nangle*, p. 340.
109 Seddall, *Nangle*, p. 348.
110 *Achill Herald*, January 1856.
111 Seddall, *Nangle*, p. 215.
112 Whelan, 'Nangle and the Achill Mission, 1834–52' in R. Gillespie & Moran (eds.), '*A various country*', *essays in Mayo history 1500–1900* (Westport, 1097), p. 133.
113 *Censuses of Ireland* for the years 1841–1901.
114 St. Thomas's Dugort, vestry minutes, 17 April 1871.
115 McNally, *Achill*, p. 101.
116 NAI, *Census of Ireland*, 1901, 125/3–5
117 Whelan, 'Nangle and the Achill Mission', p. 133.
118 Bowen, *Souperism*, p. 102.
119 Rev. William Fitzpatrick, *Achill as it is compared with what it was* (Dublin, 1886), pp 3–4.
120 Whelan, 'Nangle and the Achill Mission', p. 133.

Maynooth Research Guides for Irish Local History

IN THIS SERIES

1   Raymond Refaussé, *Church of Ireland Records*
2   Terry Dooley, *Sources for the History of Landed estates in Ireland*
3   Patrick J. Corish and David Sheehy, *Records of the Irish Catholic Church*
4   Jacinta Prunty, *Maps and Mapmaking in Local History*

Maynooth Studies in Irish Local History

IN THIS SERIES

1   Paul Connell, *Parson, Priest and Master: National Education in Co. Meath 1824–41*
2   Denis A. Cronin, *A Galway Gentleman in the Age of Improvement: Robert French of Monivea, 1716–79*
3   Brian Ó Dálaigh, *Ennis in the 18th Century: Portrait of an Urban Community*
4   Séamas Ó Maitiú, *The Humours of Donnybrook: Dublin's Famous Fair and its Suppression*
5   David Broderick, *An Early Toll-Road: The Dublin–Dunleer Turnpike, 1731–1855*
6   John Crawford, *St Catherine's Parish, Dublin 1840–1900: Portrait of a Church of Ireland Community*
7   William Gacquin, *Roscommon Before the Famine: The Parishes of Kiltoom and Cam, 1749–1845*
8   Francis Kelly, *Window on a Catholic Parish: St Mary's Granard, Co. Longford, 1933–68*
9   Charles V. Smith, *Dalkey: Society and Economy in a Small Medieval Irish Town*
10 Desmond J. O'Dowd, *Changing Times: Religion and Society in Nineteenth-Century Celbridge*
11 Proinnsíos Ó Duigneáin, *The Priest and the Protestant Woman*
12 Thomas King, *Carlow: the manor and town, 1674–1721*
13 Joseph Byrne, *War and Peace: The Survival of the Talbots of Malahide 1641–1671*
14 Bob Cullen, *Thomas L. Synnott: The Career of a Dublin Catholic 1830–70*
15 Helen Sheil, *Falling into Wretchedness: Ferbane in the late 1830s*
16 Jim Gilligan, *Graziers and Grasslands: Portrait of a Rural Meath Community 1854–1914*
17 Miriam Lambe, *A Tipperary Estate: Castle Otway, Templederry 1750–1853*
18 Liam Clare, *Victorian Bray: A Town Adapts to Changing Times*

Maynooth Studies in Irish Local History (cont.)